D1493821

Growing Remembrance

Praise for *Growing Remembrance*

'This book is the only published work chronicling the
foundation and development of this unique national tribute.'
BRITAIN AT WAR

'This is the story of the inspiration for, and the evolution of,
the National Memorial Arboretum at Alrewas in
Staffordshire by David Childs, the man who conceived the
idea and established the site. All our future military people
will have cause to thank David for his inspiration.'
PENNANT MAGAZINE

'The story of the National Memorial Arboretum is a
fascinating one.'
ROYAL AIR FORCE NEWS

Growing Remembrance

The Story of the National Memorial Arboretum

David Childs

Pen & Sword
MILITARY

First published in Great Britain in 2008 by
Pen & Sword Military

Reprinted in this format in 2011 by
Pen & Sword Military
An imprint of
Pen & Sword Books Ltd
47 Church Street
Barnsley
South Yorkshire
S70 2AS

ISBN 978 1 84884 551 0

Typeset in 11pt Palatino by
Mac Style, Beverley, E. Yorkshire
Printed and bound in the U.K.
By CPI Antony Rowe, Chippenham and Eastbourne

Pen & Sword Books Ltd incorporates the Imprints of Pen & Sword Aviation,
Pen & Sword Family History, Pen & Sword Maritime, Pen & Sword Military,
Wharncliffe Local History,
Pen & Sword Select, Pen & Sword Military Classics, Leo Cooper, Remember
When, Seaforth Publishing and Frontline Publishing

For a complete list of Pen & Sword titles please contact
PEN & SWORD BOOKS LIMITED
47 Church Street, Barnsley, South Yorkshire, S70 2AS, England
E-mail: enquiries@pen-and-sword.co.uk
Website: www.pen-and-sword.co.uk

Contents

Acknowledgements

Spread, delicate roots of my tree,
Feeling, clasping, thrusting, growing;
Sensitive pilgrim root-tips roaming everywhere
Into resistant earth your filaments forcing,
Down in the dark, unknown

Evelyn Underhill, *The Tree*

When one digs a hole, places a bare rooted tree in it, back fills and heels it in, one moment afterwards, as one stands back to check that the plant is upright and firm, the knowledge of where all those roots lie has gone. So it is with memory, especially once one has passed the age of sixty, when even remembering why one has gone upstairs can sometimes cause a difficulty. To an extent the myriad roots of the National Memorial Arboretum present a similar problem. Given the number of individuals, groups and associations involved in its establishment (making it probably the most widely supported of all Millennium project), it is not possible to recall and recount each one of those roots. Yet every one of them was important and did their bit to feed the little sapling that we planted so as to contribute to its sturdy growth. Thousands of people asked to have trees planted; hundreds of groups made donations; no corporate enterprise became a major sponsor for, given the nature of the enterprise, such sponsorship would, although welcome, have been inappropriate. The National Memorial Arboretum was grown for the nation and all had to feel a part of it if it was to achieve its purpose. So from the start it was a people's project. That having been said, the vision would not have been realized had it not had the firm blessing of the Millennium Commission, who provided nearly fifty per cent of the capital, Redland (later Lafarge) Aggregates, who donated the land, the National Forest, who awarded several tree-planting grants and helped us through many difficulties, and both Lichfield District and Staffordshire County Council, who eased our path through planning and other procedures. Without them, and in particular, Jennifer Page, Chief Executive of the Millennium Commission, Susan Bell of the National Forest, Sir Colin Corness, Chairman, and Ron Foster, Restoration Manager of Redland Aggregates, John Thompson, Chief Executive and John Colbourne, Head of Planning, at Lichfield District Council, nothing would have happened.

They made the project feasible; thousands of others were needed to make the concept a success. This is their story, and they form two intertwined trunks. Primacy must go to all those who saw in the idea of the Arboreum something appropriate to their desire to remember a loved one or pay tribute to a unit in which they served. In the early years they were committing themselves to a barren wilderness on which few trees grew and for which no funds but faith existed to transform it into a sylvan landscape worthy of their emotional and financial investment. They walked with us into this wilderness and provided the manna that kept the project alive and the vision on track. However, their trust would have been futile, had it not been for an in-house team that were able to keep us moving towards our desired destination.

Foremost among them was Jackie Fisher who in early 1995, shortly before coming District Chairman of her local Inner Wheel, selected the Arboretum, then just a concept, as her District's Charity of the Year. This act of faith in such an inchoate scheme convinced many local individuals and groups that the Arboretum was worthy of their support, and Jackie, and her husband David with his Rotary connections, made an early and most significant contribution to the project. Once her year as Chairman was over, Jackie decided that she wished to remain very involved with the Arboretum and thus began years of working untiringly both as a volunteer and then as the Site Administrator. When the Royal British Legion took the site over, Jackie stayed on as a most active fount of knowledge and expertise. It was she who established the cheerful 'can do' approach that all visitors found so welcoming and refreshing. This was also the attitude of 'The Friends of the National Memorial Arboretum', founded by Carol Daves-Lee, who provided a dedicated and delightful 'family' of helpers more than willing to undertake every task that was asked of them, as well as many that they saw needed doing and just got on with. Without such a group the project would have collapsed the first time we were ever asked to hold a major event. Through its formative years the Arboretum remained financially viable because the Friends undertook, as volunteers, many jobs that other organizations would have had to pay staff to do. Bless them all.

This book is an account of the growth of a single seed until it covered over 150 acres of land with the potential to spread further. It is neither a directory nor a guide and its length means that several individuals, organizations or groups may not find their contribution mentioned in the telling. For this I can only apologize and beg their forbearance, asking them to accept that the leaves of their trees tell their story in a far richer way than my mere words could ever do. A map displaying all the plots to date is shown at the front of the book and I hope that this will serve as an acknowledgment. But, mentioned or not, the Arboretum owes its existence to many, many thousands who were willing to put their faith in a project that had no state or corporate backing and was totally untested.

A project such as the NMA could have no blueprint for we were never certain which groups might wish to be involved and in what way they might wish their presence to be displayed. Fluid design, flexible thinking and expandable boundaries were all essential. Anthony Darbyshire of EDA showed how this might be achieved while Dan Usiskin of Architype was unpazed by being asked to design a Visitor Centre for a site with nothing to visit and no funds to pay him for his work. When those efforts turned into a funded project we needed a Project Manager and were lucky to secure the experienced services of Derek Langley, late of Chubb, who saw the building development through to its successful conclusion. Derek filled an area in which we lacked expertise, and a similar gap was filled on the financial side by first Jonathan Brown, who had managed so skilfully the closure of Leonard Cheshire's War Memorial Fund, and then by Graham Davis and Judith Thorpe. Yet while we were all beavering away on the inside, out on the site Barry Jones, with his assistant Dave Worsley, under the direction of the county arboriculturist, Paul Kennedy, was doing the really important work in planting and caring for the trees and the grounds. They also showed their faith in the project not only by committing their working days to an unestablished venture but by taking on a task that would have required the full time commitment of three times as many less energetic groundsmen.

The first person pronoun occurs very frequently in the text. The way in which the Arboretum was conceived and created makes this inevitable, but it should never be assumed that the vision could have become a reality without the participation of the thousands referred to above. They made it happen. They were not involved because of any charismatic leadership, brilliant blueprint or unstoppable band wagon that they needed to board. The reverse is probably, no definitely, true. Having seen the vision they saw that their involvement was imperative if this promising sapling was not to wither and die. They were the husbandmen and it was their nurturing that made it grow.

Finally, this book could not have been published without the enthusiastic support of those presently working at the National Memorial Arboretum, in particular, the director, Charlie Bagot-Jewett, his assistant Helen Overton, who supplied many of the photographs. Finally, to Henry Wilson and his team at Pen & Sword, especially my editor, George Chamier, I extend my gratitude and, I hope, that of the readership.

Foreword by
HRH The Prince of Wales

In October 2007 I was greatly moved to attend the dedication of the Armed Forces Memorial at the National Memorial Arboretum. This imposing structure, listing the 16,000 names of all those members of the armed and merchant services who have lost their lives in conflicts since the end of the Second World War, serves to remind us of the price that has been paid for the peace most of us have enjoyed for over sixty years.

Earlier in the last century, when that peace and the freedom that went with it was under the greatest threat, millions responded to save our Nation's life; hundreds of thousands did not return home, many more were injured in body and mind, thousands endured a harsh captivity. We, the generation that was born just after the end of the Second World War, owe them a debt that can never be repaid. The creation of the National Memorial Arboretum, by acknowledging that debt through the planting of trees, not only pays tribute to those who were prepared to give so much, but also gifts to the future a place of beauty and joy. More than this, each dedicated tree, every memorial, tells a story that should never be forgotten. History books or lessons alone cannot do this: they simply do not have the space nor time, but wandering through the wide acres of this Arboretum encourages visitors to seek out those tales themselves. The stories they reveal are many and varied, and always thrilling.

Although the National Memorial Arboretum fulfils the national purpose, it was created neither by Government decree nor committee. Instead, a small group of men and women, having decided that there was a debt of honour to a whole generation that needed to be repaid, got together with many Service and Veteran's organizations to turn an idea into reality. For centuries to come their vision will continue to grow and bring a reflective pleasure to all who walk beneath the trees in peace and freedom. Year upon year memories inevitably fade, but here at the National Memorial Arboretum the memorials linked to them will flourish. That is its genius and its joy.

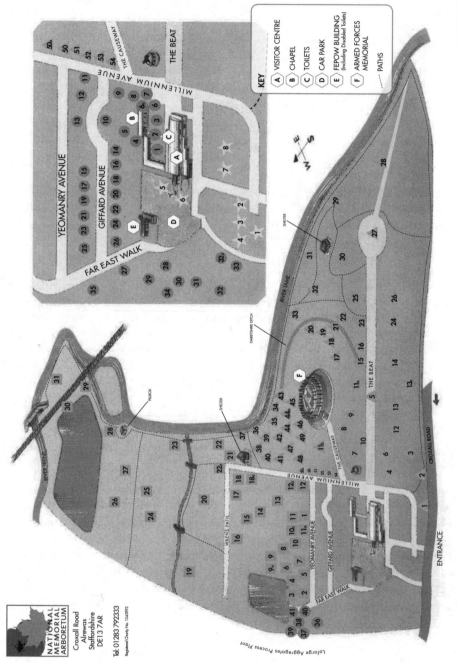

© The National Memorial Arboretum

KEY

- **A** VISITOR CENTRE
- **B** CHAPEL
- **C** TOILETS
- **D** CAR PARK
- **E** FEPOW BUILDING (Including Disabled Toilets)
- **F** ARMED FORCES MEMORIAL
- - - - - PATHS

NATIONAL MEMORIAL ARBORETUM

Croxall Road
Alrewas
Staffordshire
DE13 7AR

Tel: 01283 792333

Registered Charity No. 1043992

Dedicated to all who contributed so much to the creation of the National Memorial Arboretum and who now look down on the leaves

Introduction

The Unrepayable Debt

Nature provides the best monument.
The perfecting of the work must be
left to the gentle hand of time,
but each returning Spring will bring
a fresh tribute to those whom it is
desired to keep in everlasting remembrance.

Lines from a war memorial on Wimbledon Common near Putney

The old have borne most; we that are young
Will never see as much or live as long.

William Shakespeare, *King Lear*, closing lines

This is a story about creation and the people who were present both to witness it and to assist at its birth – people whose lives, losses, triumphs and disasters, memories, dreams and gifts have been commemorated and celebrated through the planting of trees. Their combined experiences are the weft and warp of British history through the twentieth century. Their combined action will ensure that their story remains forever green. No one plants a tree for their own benefit; it is planted so that it might be enjoyed by those who are young, even as yet unborn. Those who planted the trees in the National Memorial Arboretum did so mainly as a tribute to those who had borne much and as a gift for the future to enjoy and reflect upon. We who did the planting are thus the least important part of that trunk whose roots stretch back into the twentieth century and whose leaves will one day open to greet a twenty-second century Spring dawn. By that time some hundred thousand trees may have been planted, each one a tribute to one, two, a dozen, a hundred, a thousand or more individuals. We who planted them can only hope that we might spend eternity gazing down at those leaves rather than up at the roots, while those for whom they were planted walk in their dappled shade enjoying life in a nation at peace with itself and its neighbours.

The trees were planted as a living tribute to all who served their country in an age of violence which saw the British nation at war or in conflict for most of the past hundred years. Yet, out of these troubled times was born a generation most of whom lived their lives if not in total peace, certainly in freedom. But it was a freedom bought at a great price. Two world wars secured for the inhabitants of our islands a life without tyranny and misrule, a life of liberty and increasing prosperity. Yet, for this freedom, some two million British and Commonwealth men and women lost their lives, while many more were blighted by injury, both mental and physical, or the loss of loved ones.

The members of that generation who came safe home spent much time and effort erecting memorials to their fallen colleagues. Every year we, their children, would listen, at first, and then watch as they marched past the Cenotaph each November. Even those of us who knew not the hardships that they had endured felt the solemnity of that moment. Only with our maturing years did we appreciate that the sacrifices that had been made were for our future, although we were as yet unborn. Only as we moved through and beyond the Cold War into our middle age did we appreciate that, thanks to them, we had been part of the luckiest generation ever to have been born in Britain. Without them our life could have been a lot different and a lot worse. We are in debt to those who were prepared to put their lives at risk so that we might be free, and we who owe the most need to remember the most, for the debt itself is unrepayable.

The enormity of that debt and the fact that it could never be repaid was brought to my attention by Group Captain Leonard (later Lord) Cheshire VC, OM, DSO**. Leonard felt that we should all be involved in ensuring that the sacrifice of the many should never be forgotten. Possessing as he did the modesty of a generation who belittled their own contribution, believing that their survival was recognition and reward enough, Leonard's mind was firmly fixed on remembering those who had died in war. But we who came after owed our very existence to those who had come safely home and started to build from the rubble a world in which we could live in peace. We, the post war generation, had done nothing significant as a group to say thank you to our parents' generation and we needed to do so before they too marched away to join that army which no man can number. We also had our own youngsters who, twice removed from the great conflicts, probably needed to be reminded of the debt even more than did we.

And it had to be us. So many of that war time generation could not conceive that their own contribution should be worthy of note. A gentle modesty combined with the memory of those who were not growing old made them consider survival was acknowledgement enough. They would agree with Shakespeare's words in King Lear: 'To be remembered is o'er paid'.

It was for us to disprove that sentiment, for remembrance is the smallest repayment that we are able to make.

With the imminent arrival of a new millennium being preceded by the end of the Cold War the world faced its future with hope. Our tribute to the past needed to reflect that hope for the future, and there seemed no better way to do this than through the planting of trees – trees in honour of an entire past generation, planted by the present one to give something of beauty and reflection for a generation to come. Thus was born the concept of a National Memorial Arboretum.

CHAPTER ONE

Millennium Limes: From Vision to Reality

These are the trees whose hidden flowers of fawn
Spill on the air a perfume sweet and strong,
Sought by the bees, who to their riches throng
From bowers of lavender and roses drawn ...
Silent I stood, for from those perfect Limes
Flamed God's fair answer to this sad world's crimes.

F. M. Ward

Group Captain Leonard (later Lord) Cheshire VC, OM, DSO**, through the bravery that made him Britain's most highly decorated airman and the compassion that led to his founding of the eponymous homes and services for the disabled, is probably everyone's idea of a hero. Couple his achievements with his simple and unshakeable faith in the teachings of the Roman Catholic Church and he would probably top any poll to nominate a British Saint for the twentieth century. Yet this man of action was also both a visionary and a lateral thinker.

Towards the end of his life, Leonard Cheshire became concerned with the slow response that the United Nations and its member states were making to what seemed to be the increasing number of natural disasters that were occurring throughout the world. Famines in the Horn of Africa, earthquakes in Iran and Armenia, none seemed to be met with the urgency that was needed if their worst effects on the survivors were to be mitigated. For Leonard, who shared the general euphoria linked to the ending of the Cold War, natural disasters and the humanitarian response to them were going to replace conflict resolution as the main challenge facing the world in the new century. They needed to be addressed with all the dedication and determination with which nations had stood up to the challenge of a century of violence.

But in Leonard's own century, the greatest global disasters had been man made: two world wars that had accounted for, at a conservative estimate, some eighty million lives. He was, therefore, also, concerned that we should not forget this horror and the debt so many owed to those who had given their lives that others might live.

So Leonard Cheshire united these two ideas. He saw that the world possessed sufficient food, manpower and material to respond instantly to an disaster. What was needed to speed matters up was either ready money or a guarantee that funds would be forthcoming. Delays caused by haggling over cost were wholly unacceptable, but from where was this instant access money to come? The answer, in Leonard's mind, was to create a fund so enormous that the interest alone would be sufficient to fund any disaster relief operation that could be anticipated. And the way to encourage people to help create such a fund was to ask them to give five pounds in remembrance of each life that had been lost in the two greatest disasters the world had ever experienced. Leonard linked these two concepts with a short catch phrase:

'Remember a Life to Save a Life'

and he created a Charity, 'The World Memorial Fund for Disaster Relief' (WMF) to administer the project. He little realised that this catch phrase would lead to the creation of the largest memorial in this country to all those lost lives he so revered. Such an outcome was far from his mind as, using his formidable reputation, he went to see those at the highest level of Government. Soon he had the Secretary General of the United Nations and many heads of state agreeing to his idea. Agree they might, but helping fund it was an entirely different matter. If the WMF was to make a difference then Leonard Cheshire was going to have to raise the monies himself. As ever, with a philosophy founded on the unshakeable belief that 'God would provide', Leonard set off to raise four hundred million pounds!

While Leonard was developing his ideas for a WMF, I was endeavouring to get the Ministry of Defence interested in becoming involved in Disaster Relief operations, although my interest was not purely humanitarian. I was concerned that, with both conflict and threat diminishing, opportunities to give service personnel the experience and training that they needed to keep them honed to the highest standard were also reducing. The best theatre in which professional skills could be tested was in the area of Disaster Relief where planners, logisticians, aviators, communicators, engineers and medics could all find themselves having to respond to a crisis that mimicked but was not war. This was especially important for the medical services, who in peace time exercises had to be content with dealing with a casualty whose only indications of injury were a label tied around a limb announcing 'broken leg' and some badly applied ghoulish make up. If a real casualty occurred then the exercise stopped, to be replaced by a Board of Enquiry. Morale also suffered. It was difficult to retain skilled personnel if their civilian peer group were building roads and bridges or providing field-hospitals for real in response to a disaster, while they erected temporary structures on Salisbury Plain. The problem for me was that, although the uniformed professionals were very enthusiastic, the Ministry of Defence civil servants were not and, what is more, they refused to budge from charging the Overseas Development Agency (ODA) such high hire costs that Service involvement` was priced out of the market whenever that agency requested support. However, with someone as well respected as Leonard Cheshire behind the idea then attitudes might be changed. I went to see him.

Meeting someone with as wonderful a reputation as Leonard Cheshire is rather like a rehearsal for meeting Saint Peter. My nerves were not aided by the fact that I was to be introduced at a small meeting at which his wife, the equally remarkable but formidable Sue Ryder, was also present. Leonard, however, possessed the gift not only of making a visitor immediately at ease but also of making them think that he had nothing better to do with his time than to listen to their opinions. He could cast bread on the waters and sit back and watch the fish gather his crumbs. I must have made some impression because two days later I was summoned by my boss to be told that the First Sea Lord had just been called by Leonard Cheshire and 'told' [sic] that I was to be released from the Royal Navy to go and work for him. Much embarrassed, I returned to my office to ring Leonard and tell him that he had got the wrong end of the stick but that, when my circumstances changed, I promised I would work for his new charity which I thought was a brilliant idea. In the meantime, I would do what I could from my small corner where the plans for Service involvement in Disaster Relief Operations grew apace while the desire of the MoD civil servants to encourage or implement them remained at best lukewarm.

Leonard Cheshire was never daunted by the scale of the task he had set himself, but he realised that there was one factor over which he had no control – his age. If WMF was to become a practical answer in his lifetime to the shortcomings he was witnessing, then it needed to raise serious money rapidly. Money was trickling in from hundreds of donors but most of them were of Leonard's generation and loved the idea of giving five pounds to remember the life of a relative or loved one. Many could not afford anything more. The letters that came with these five pound notes often brought tears to the eyes. The secretarial support that was necessary, for every letter was replied to in a personal way, was considerable, while the growth of the fund from these thousands of donors was infinitesimally small and too slow to stand a chance of reaching Leonard's ambitious target. A big event was needed, which is where it all went wrong.

In 1990 Leonard became involved with the backing of a major rock concert to be held in Berlin where Pink Floyd were to perform their epic 'The Wall'. The band, very generously, had agreed to have the profit from what was planned to be the largest such gathering in history donated to the Fund. If that had been the limit of WMF's involvement all would have been well, but somehow the Fund became involved in the organisation of the event, a situation that rapidly led to the concert being underwritten by the charity's business arm. With neither a professional manager nor any control on expenditure, money disappeared and at the end of a concert which had met every target, WMF was very significantly in the red, or rather the business that had been set up to manage the concert on WMF's behalf was. After several years of trying to build up a major Fund, Leonard was further away from his vision than when he had started. It broke him and, always frail, he began to wilt. In 1992 he was to write about the problems of the WMF, 'Nothing in my forty-two years of working in the field of charity has worried me as much as this.' On 31 July 1992 he died.

Sadly and ironically, a few months after Leonard's death I found myself in a position either to act upon or ignore my earlier promise to him to help establish WMF. The armed forces were beginning a process of manpower reduction, and it was obvious to me that my services would shortly no longer be required. The question was, with Leonard gone and his fund in severe crisis, did my promise to him still hold good? I believed that it did but then a second question arose, which was whether or not WMF still existed as a going concern. If the Charity had become established there would have been no question; I believed passionately in its cause and the logic behind the idea. But a debit balance of two million pounds was not a healthy way to start a new career running a fund that was meant to disperse monies to meet major disasters.

My thinking had, however, moved on. Although I was never able to discuss the matter with Leonard there seemed to me to be a disjunction between remembering lives lost in combat and supporting disaster relief operations. This was uncomfortable because Leonard's whole idea, his wonderful slogan, depended on this combination of 'remembering a life' and 'saving a life.' This was an urgent issue, for the financially crippled WMF was not, in the foreseeable future, going to make any contribution whatsoever to disaster relief. Moreover, those who had given money for this purpose, were going to have to be informed, either that their contribution had been absorbed by a pop concert or that some new, more sustainable and achievable idea had replaced the original concept. In a nutshell, what could a Charity with no funds contribute as a player in an area where, without funding, nothing could be achieved? I believed that

I had an idea but it would involve a drastic rethink of Leonard's original concept. On the afternoon of 25 September, following Leonard's memorial service in Westminster Cathedral, I met up with the WMF Trustees (Sir Peter Ramsbotham, Baroness Sue Ryder and David Puttnam), who had gathered to begin the process of closing down the charity, to tell them that Leonard's vision could be saved but that I needed an entirely free hand to apply some of the lateral thinking for which its founder was so justly renowned. They approved.

It was lucky that my involvement in planning and interest in disaster relief had led to my being reasonably well informed as to the real needs of both man-made and natural disasters. The world community had advanced quite significantly since the tragedies of the Armenian and Iranian earthquakes had led to Leonard setting up the WMF in response. In the early nineties we all got a large dose of political euphoria: after all, the Cold War was coming to an end and a new millennium would herald in a golden age of peace as men at last heeded the words of the Christmas carol:

> Beneath the angels' strain have rolled
> Two thousand years of wrong
> And man at war with man hears not
> The love song that they bring
> Oh! hush your noise ye men of strife
> And hear the angels sing.

Sadly, as the millennium approached, arrived and passed on, war and conflict visited the earth with far greater moment than the arrival of the Prince of Peace, and the angels' song remained unheard.

Many of these conflicts were reducing communities towards the absolute zero of medical care. TV screens were filled night after night with pictures of the injured lying in basements where hard pressed surgeons tried to operate under paraffin lamps while gunfire echoed around them. Medics throughout the country responded to the obvious need and got themselves despatched to the war zone; communities throughout the land organised food and clothing convoys; schools held collections; politicians pronounced and ... the WMF did nothing, could not do anything. Or could it?

We were giving advice and some guidance but we had very limited skills and it was while analysing this lack that the answer came forward. During discussions with a great friend, Colonel Jim Ryan, the Professor of Military Surgery in the RAMC, we worked out that it was not while the bullets were flying that devastated or newly formed countries needed support but, paradoxically, once the conflict was over. The UN, NGOs, volunteers were always available to support those under siege, but once peace was restored many of these pulled out leaving a country whose medical and caring infrastructure, along with most other structures, had been devastated. Our analysis had also shown that even those with horrific injuries could pull through if reasonably competent medical care was available, but very often they were hastily sewn up or repaired like badly stuck together bone china; without physiotherapy or subsequent surgery they would become disabled and unemployed just at a time when their nation needed as many able bodied people as it could muster to assist with reconstruction.

What we felt was needed was support in Conflict Recovery, our new concept of a multi-skilled discipline in which a few highly skilled professionals working alongside their local opposite numbers might achieve a great deal. But where to get these professionals and how to fund them? University was the obvious answer and here we were lucky. Jim had just been appointed Director of A&E at University College London Hospital where the experience he had gained in his army career, plus the Service's emphasis on trauma care, were needed in an area that has never been glamorous to NHS professionals but which, nevertheless, needed a high degree of skill. His job gave him time to devote attention to the study of 'Conflict Recovery'. All we needed to do was fund it.

Armed with the concept of 'Conflict Recovery' as a definable discipline, and Leonard Cheshire's name as an entrée, I called on the Dean at the University to discuss the establishment of a professorial chair. While the logic for doing this was willingly received and the advantages to basing it at the University with Jim Ryan at its head clearly agreed, funding was a different issue. How much? The minimum needed was put at £250,000, which was £236,000 more than we had. I offered the £14,000 as a down payment – an approach which was acknowledged as original – and retired with an invitation to bring a few of my Trustees to dinner to firm matters up.

The Chairman of WMF was a wonderful gentleman. Sir Peter Ramsbotham had been the British Ambassador in Washington and had got to know Leonard Cheshire after his own daughter had suffered an horrific accident and become a resident of one of Leonard's Homes. Soon he was actively involved with Leonard's charities and became chairman of the Ryder Cheshire Foundation. He was, from my point of view, an excellent Chairman of WMF, recognising its past failure and keen to support anything that could save Leonard's idea, however far it might have to stray from the original concept. Peter recognised in the proposal for the 'Leonard Cheshire Chair of Conflict Recovery' an idea that might work, made sense and would have appealed to Leonard. He charmed our hosts and the Chair was established. Now we only had to pay for it. In its initial few years we just managed to have the money available at the end of each month to meet our wage bills; demands for rental of our premises and other costs were met through negotiation rather than notes. It was all we were in a position to do. One week after I had taken on the WMF job, the philanthropist who had been sponsoring the fund's administrative expenses withdrew his support, indicating that he was doing so as it had no viable future. A great way to start a new career! Our expenses had to be met with what money was forthcoming from the ever diminishing royalties from 'The Wall' CD and merchandising, as well as a modest contribution from the other element of Leonard Cheshire's WMF motto, 'Remember a Life'.

The idea of the World Memorial Fund had been launched by Leonard in a radio broadcast. The money that came in was mainly from people of his own wartime generation, many of whom, so great was the reverence in which he was held, would have marched over a cliff if he had so commanded. But most people still wished to see something tangible as a memorial to a loved one; a bank account, however, large was never going to be tribute enough.

One of my service tasks was, in time of war, to serve as part of a British liaison team on the staff of the Supreme Allied Commander Atlantic at his Norfolk, Virginia, Headquarters. This meant twice yearly trips to Norfolk, via Washington, for exercises. On one of these I found myself with a spare Saturday in Washington before my return flight on the Monday. It was a lovely day and I spent the morning walking through Arlington Military Cemetery where the graves lie between wonderful lines of trees. In the afternoon I visited the National Arboretum and spent the rest of the day wandering around this 450 acre collection of beautiful and exotic trees. I returned to my hotel with my legs protesting at the miles they had covered that day.

In the night I woke up with the two places I had visited combined in my mind – a National Memorial Arboretum where tribute to those who had lost their lives defending our country's future could be made by planting a tree, a living symbol of a future of hope.

On the flight home – serendipity! There, in a copy of *The Daily Telegraph*, was an article about a Government initiative to create a National Forest to be sited in the counties of Leicestershire, Derbyshire and Staffordshire and through major tree planting to help cover up and heal the scars from centuries of mining and other mineral extraction. This struck me immediately as the best scheme for the betterment of the English landscape in the whole of the twentieth century. It seemed obvious that this was where any National Memorial Arboretum would have to be.

When I got back home I wrote a letter to the inchoate organisation that was coming together to form a staff for The National Forest. This small team was going to be responsible for encouraging landowners, villages, councils, individuals to plant millions of trees. To prepare the ground they were going to be able to give grants for planting, but their best incentive was their own enthusiasm and in their leader, Susan Bell, they had a charming, persuasive and very competent advocate. Susan was determined that the project would succeed and, even when its future was in doubt, she exuded the confidence that persuaded all who came into contact with her and her team that nothing was going to stop their vision of greening the Midlands and creating a new forest for the benefit of all.

It took a while after my original letter for me to be able to call on Susan Bell and talk through my ideas with her. This was a critical meeting, for if she had not been supportive, then we were unlikely to succeed, especially as I lived over 150 miles from The National Forest and would therefore need to work with those better placed and better informed than me. Susan placed herself and her team right behind the idea, for not only could she see what a valuable asset the proposed arboretum would be to the National Forest but as her father had been killed in Korea she had a very personal sense of what we were trying to achieve.

There were three organisations whose support at the very beginning would be essential if the idea of the NMA was to become a reality: these were The National Forest, Lichfield District Council and Redland Aggregates. The project was blessed in that the key players in each of these organisations greeted the idea with enthusiasm and had a 'can do' approach to its development. This latter was important for they would be dealing, in me, with someone who had no experience of estate management, planning, fundraising or planting; indeed, for most of my career close contact with a tree would have meant something had gone seriously wrong with my navigation.

Unlike any of the other groups involved with The National Forest, we were neither land owners nor investors. We needed to find some land before we could even become involved, and to make it that more difficult, I was convinced that it had to be free land, for I believed we could not hope to ask people to raise the purchase price of a park before they could even consider planting a tree. We needed at least 100 acres and we needed it free.

Faced with the task of finding a very generous landowner, I ignored the problem and procrastinated by writing to several of the great and good to invite them to become Patrons of this new project. Very few turned the invitation down, and two proved to be instrumental in securing us our land.

As part of their support for the NMA, the National Forest organised a walk around some land on the East bank of the River Tame that had recently been restored by Redland Aggregates after gravel extraction. This wedge-shaped plot, hemmed in by a railway line, a river and a lake, could only be approached either through a gap in the railway viaduct or from a bend in the main road. It was also badly drained and marshy although it did have its own beautiful lake in one corner. The gravel pit had been in filled with pulverised fuel ash from the nearby power station, and no one was sure how that would affect young tree roots, although it was having no effect on a wonderful specimen of Black Poplar, Populus nigra var. betulifolia, growing nearby. Further disadvantages also lay under the ground, for the site was crisscrossed by high pressure gas pipe lines. Yet the site had one overriding virtue. As we walked round the field it became apparent that the Redland representative, Tim Sporne, was prepared to consider, subject to authorisation, leasing the land for free. A swift follow-up was needed.

Among the people whom I had recruited as Patrons was the President of the Royal Horticultural Society, Sir Simon Hornby. When I looked up Sir Colin Corness, the Chairman of Redland Aggregates, in Who's Who, his business posts and clubs rang a bell; they were the same as Sir Simon's. I therefore rang him and asked him if he knew Colin Corness. He did and, what was more, would be seeing him at dinner in a few days time. I suggested that if the conversation dried up he might ask whether or not Redland might give us the site for free. I am sure that the conversation flowed well, but a few days later Redland made us an offer of a 999 year lease at a nominal rent of £1 a year. The terms would stipulate that if the rent were to be in arrears for 21 days it would be considered a breach of the lease and that Redland could then regain possession of the site. From then on I always made sure that I had a pound coin in my pocket as I walked around the site in case anyone from Redland, later Lafarge, demanded settlement.

So we had some land which, I kept convincing myself, was ideal for the Arboretum. We next required permission to transform it into an Arboretum and for this we needed the support and approval of Lichfield District Council.

The first recollection that I had of the word 'Midlands' was listening to my mother read Belloc's poem The South Country with its couplet:

> When I am living in the Midlands
> That are sodden and unkind

Years of planting the Arboretum demonstrated how truly Belloc spoke with his first adjective; the second could not have been further from the truth, for Lichfield District Council was staffed with those who proved Belloc wrong. Once more we were blessed. Lichfield, a jewel of a cathedral city, lies, for anyone travelling from the South, behind the great rain shadow of Birmingham. With the M1 on one side and the M6 on the other there is no reason for the traveller to discover the city, especially for those wishing to avoid the snarl-up that so often delays journeys even without detours. But not to visit is to miss out on that fairest of cathedrals, the Lady of the Vale, with her warm red sandstone walls and her three fine spires. For my purposes, Lichfield was ideal. It possessed a District Council in its own right so with the authority to make relevant decisions and yet it was a small enough Council and city for everyone to know everyone else and for no officer or councillor to be too remote. I soon got to know the Chief Executive, John Thompson who years later we were to discover was related to my wife's family, and his Head of Planning, John Colborne. Through all the period of development I cannot recall one obstacle which the two Johns did not either provide an answer to or propose an acceptable way round. Their enthusiasm and support was reflected by the Council seeing obvious advantages in a national attraction being created within their boundaries, and they were understanding and flexible enough to listen to a disorganised team of one who neither knew the area nor had existing funds to pour immediately into the scheme.

The scheme itself had to be a flexible one. With the lessons of the Berlin rock concert and with no experience of handling public donations, I wanted to make sure that money given was spent where it was intended and that we should not commit ourselves to projects which we could not afford. The proposal for the Arboretum was therefore staged depending on the level of funds raised. Firstly, we planned to create a woodland with copses linked to organisations and trees named for individuals; then, when funds permitted, we would build a small visitor information centre, followed, when we could afford it, by the creation of a larger visitor centre and more specialist plots.

When we started, it was with that first stage very much in mind. My assistant, Ada Doyle, who had worked with WMF, produced all the correspondence with those who had supported Leonard's original idea, and we wrote to every one of them. They were not easy letters for we not only had to explain the fading of Leonard's vision but also had to convince them that our idea, built upon his foundation, of a Chair of Conflict Recovery and a National Memorial Arboretum was both a logical and legitimate heir; also that it would work and that giving money to have a dedicated tree planted would not be making a contribution towards another failure. The response was better than we anticipated. We had no letters of reproach and a large number of donations, the general flavour of which can be gleaned from the following short notes:

Last weekend, as we made a family pilgrimage to his grave and his grand-children thrust already drooping flowers into the soggy earth, someone said, 'It's a pity we can't plant a tree; he loved his trees! And now this opportunity!

What a splendid idea ... as a member of the Society of Friends and someone concerned with the environment it has a double appeal.

I would like a tree planted in memory of Flying Officer Ian Sutherland who died over Germany in 1940. He was the only man that I ever could have married and so I remain, Yours Sincerely, Miss—

Receiving letters like these made us realize how much this project was going to mean to so many people and how much faith was being put in our achieving the stated aim. The response also gave us the confidence to set up The National Memorial Arboretum as a charity independent of WMF, an action that would give us the added advantage of being able to close down this now moribund trust. Registering a charity and a limited company with no funds and the word 'National' in its title gave rise to several additional questions, but at least the Trustees of the WMF were willing to stay on. In fact they split, with Sir Peter Ramsbotham chairing the Leonard Cheshire Chair of Conflict Recovery and David Puttnam (later Lord Puttnam of Queensgate) chairing the NMA. The move coincided with David Puttnam's increasing and time consuming involvement with the world of politics but throughout 'he remained involved and available to discuss the Arboretum and to act as its advocate. He was seldom able to stay long at Trustee meetings but he always left promising to sort out or deliver two or three issues. The next day Valerie, his excellent PA , would telephone to say that he had done what had been asked of him. David Puttnam also recruited two friends to serve as additional Trustees, one of whom, Sir Graham Hearne, Chairman of Enterprise Oil, was able to arrange a donation that arrived at one of our critical cash flow moments, thus saving us from a major embarrassment. David also wrote to the Duchess of Kent, who was another personal friend, to ask her to be our royal patron. She agreed and provided joy and charm, interest and concern at the highest level.

The big breakthrough for the NMA came with the Government's announcement of the setting up of a National Lottery. Although our aims and objectives had been established well before its creation they matched perfectly those laid down for the Millennium Commission branch of the Lottery so we did not, like many organisations, have to create or amend an existing project to qualify for support. Our position was different; we had a good idea but would the Commissioners and their staff be convinced that we were capable enough to deliver it? We put in an initial letter of interest and were summoned to meet a project officer.

When I arrived, the Millennium Commission staff viewed me with some concern and asked whether my colleagues had been delayed. I explained that I was a team of one but in possession of a good idea. After several eyebrows had been raised we got down to business. Worryingly, I had to confess that I had neither funds nor fundraising experience, had never planted a single tree and had a staff of two to deliver the project. I expected to be dismissed but they heard me out, asked straightforward questions and, finally, invited me to draw up an application for support. I left, several sweated pounds lighter but convinced that we would get a fair hearing from the Commissioners and Jenny Page, their Chief Executive, regardless of our size and lack of experience because the strength of our vision was capable of carrying us forward.

This early encouragement led to a move to launch the project through a national appeal, and an approach to the Prime Minister, John Major, kindly organised by The National Forest, drew a positive response. The Prime Minister was prepared to give a press launch in early November, the closest date that he had available to Remembrance Sunday. I drafted a speech and forwarded it to his office and, straight after PM's question time on 1 November 1994, with my notes in his hand, he strode up to the dais in front of the journalists who had assembled in the House of Commons. My draft was put to one side and never looked at; instead the Prime Minister spoke for 15 minutes without notes, hesitation, repetition or deviation about his own love of trees and how much he thought our idea was a valuable one. The speech also included a few lines that we were to use at the start of our application and business plans submitted to the Millennium Commission. These were:

I think it will be a fitting, a remarkable and a sympathetic memorial to those people who suffered in war and to their families both in the short term and the long term. Many of us here, perhaps none of us, will be around when the memorial reaches its full beauty. But future generations will be including the future generations of those people whose gallantry it marks and they will be able to see this remarkable memorial as it flowers for a generation yet to come.

In those few words the Prime Minister got to the core of what the developing aim of the Arboretum was to become. We hoped that the Millennium Commission and their officials would read the Prime Minister's words and realise that our project was very close and true to the spirit of their work. The one difficulty that we were going to have with the Commission was that our vision, as the Prime Minister made clear, looked far into the future, much farther, we sometimes felt, than the Commission staff seemed to do themselves, for we got very strange looks when we told them that 1 January 2000 was not a significant milestone in our activities although 1 January 2100 might be! Few plant trees believing that they will be around to witness the mature plant in its crowning glory; they do so as a gift to the future. Thus the Arboretum was to be a tribute to the past and a gift to the future, with the present generation acting as a bridge across the years. This concept became encapsulated in the project's slogan:

Remember the Future

which was very close to one conceived shortly afterwards by The Royal British Legion (TRBL):

Remember the past, but don't forget the future

an important similarity, for I foresaw that if the Arboretum was to succeed we would need the involvement of that organisation whose vision of a duty of remembrance so matched our own.

So, as our confidence grew we were able to focus our defining aims. These became:

To establish an Arboretum of sufficient size and stature to serve as a living national symbol of Remembrance and Reconciliation for the generations affected by the wars of this [the twentieth] century and to be a gift in their memory for future generations to reflect upon and enjoy.

While these administrative ground preparations were being put in place we were also talking to Forest Enterprise at Westonbirt Arboretum about a design for the project, and they, like so many of the early supporters, were prepared to draw one up pro bono. The support from the team at Westonbirt, and from all arboriculturists that we came in contact with, was never less than enthusiastic and they were all very willing to make allowances for my complete lack of professional knowledge.

It was through a suggestion made at Westonbirt that the Arboretum gained one of its most impressive features. I had wanted to create a long Avenue to signify the two thousand years of the Millennium and had thought that we should plant it with trees with a known longevity, but could only think of yew and redwood, neither of which would have been appropriate. Westonbirt got me to think backwards. In their Silk Wood there is a circular stand of sixty small-leafed limes, *Tilia cordata*, created from a single plant as a result of centuries of coppicing. It was never considered that this fifty foot diameter circle of trees could possibly be one specimen until DNA fingerprinting proved it to be so. Some experts consider that the stand might date back 6,000 years which could give it a link with Britain's most famous ancient monument, Stonehenge. Thousands of years ago the stripped bark of lime trees was soaked and woven to form rope and it was with cords made of lime that the stones that came from Wales to Wiltshire to be erected as part of Stonehenge would have been dragged across the countryside. Given the location of Silk Wood in Gloucestershire, these old limes may have been a part of an agro-factory making ropes for this purpose. Westonbirt agreed to take cuttings from this lime to plant as our Millennium Avenue. It was a very proud day when they were eventually brought to the Arboretum for planting. Sadly, several were lost through both water-logging in a series of bad winters and by crow damage, for every winter when the plants were brittle crows seemed unable to resist landing on them and snapping them off – it was the only form of vandalism that the Arboretum was to suffer. Luckily, of course, as long as the Silk Wood flourishes replacements will be available to ensure the Avenue's trees date back genetically to a time when, in Blake's vision, the man whose life they commemorated had walked upon England's mountains green.

Buoyed up by Lichfield District Council's enthusiasm we put in for initial planning permission for a change of land use. We were in for a shock but one for which I should have been prepared; permission was opposed by the Health & Safety Executive because of the spider's web of gas pipe, lines running under the site each of which required a regulatory exclusion zone on either side. I was unable to accept that their objections were not insurmountable through careful and cunning redesign and spent several weeks coming up with new ideas for the layout and presenting them to the HSE for comment. They were kind, helpful, unimpressed and unmoveable. Suddenly, euphoria evaporated and we were, thanks to my poor planning, back where I had insisted we should never be, in receipt of funds for a project we could not deliver. There was just one glimmer of hope.

When Redland had first offered the site their very experienced Restoration Manager, Ron Foster, had suggested that we would be better to consider the other side of the river which Redland had also recently restored. I had paid little attention to this but now rang Ron and explained the situation to him. Remarking that at last I had come to my senses, Ron set in train the arrangements to lease us the new site. Agreement was reached very quickly and, although the land lay alongside Redland's ongoing gravel works it had every advantage over the first site, including both access and room for expansion as well as an infill that was inert and not made up of pulverised fuel ash.

There is no doubt that had planning permission been granted for the initial site the development of the Arboretum would have been halted at some stage. Now, thanks to the combined efforts of Health & Safety and Redland Aggregates, we were on the site where we should always have been. We didn't tell John Major but I had to inform Jennifer Page, who had been both probing and positive on her visit to the site, that despite my persuasive enthusiasm for the original location, I was now convinced that we had a better one. She acquiesced.

The rules of the Millennium Commission at this time stated that they would support capital projects. Planting trees did not qualify as a capital project. Thus we had to refine our approach if we were to qualify for this major source of funding and, as the only feasible capital work we could consider was a Visitor Centre, this was something we were forced to turn our minds to. Most established arboreta in this country began with the planting of trees which, as they matured, attracted visitors in such numbers that it was necessary to provide some sort of information centre and then a complete visitor centre. Neither Westonbirt nor Stourhead, with their lofty centuries-old collections of trees had, at the time that we were planning our project, adequate visitor centres and yet we, with no trees planted, were planning a major building. It seemed strange but it was going to be necessary.

There was logic that suggested that a visitor centre for an Arboretum should be both built of wood and sustainable, but how to go about finding an architect? A colleague working on a different project from the same office drew my attention to an article about the London Wildlife Centre which had been built with these principles by a firm, called Architype, whose offices were not far away at London Bridge. I contacted them and arranged to meet two partners, Jonathan Hind and Dan Usiskin. Over a beer I explained that I had no experience, no funds, inadequate resources, no lease and no guarantee of Millennium Commission support. The two partners looked at each other, drank their beer, looked at me and said 'That seems fine when do we start?'

There was no doubt that so committed were Architype to the creation of sustainable, environmentally friendly buildings (an area in which they bemoaned the UK was so far behind the Scandinavians) that they were keen to grasp any opportunity to create such a building. Our visitor centre appealed to them, so much so that they were prepared, crucially, to provide an initial design pro bono, on the understanding that should it be approved they would be contracted to do the work. This was not only an admirable arrangement but the only one that would convince the Millennium Commission we were capable of producing and funding a design within the time constraints that the Commission was placing upon every project. Yet even after the agreement with Architype was in place we were still faced with a number of problems.

Firstly, most of the land that Redland had originally agreed to lease to us lay within the flood plain of the River Tame, with ony a small area lying above the hundred year flood mark. This gave us sufficient space on which to build a visitor centre but not our Millennium Chapel which, from the start, I had felt would be an appropriate edifice to raise at the site, given both the timing of the project and the purpose for which it was intended. How we were going to ensure that the Chapel did not flood regularly was one of the first of a number of searching questions that the Commission posed . This one came with a tight time frame. On the way down from London to home, having been faced with this question, I sketched a plan for a floating Chapel. This was based around a series of wooden piles to which the Chapel, built upon a raft, would be attached so that it would rise up with the water level. It looked interesting and would have had great visitor appeal. We immediately referred to it as 'The Ark', but we were spared any blushes that might have resulted from its failure to float by the change of site to one which included a strip of higher land. Even then flooding could have been a problem. The Environment Agency could not confirm whether or not our building footprint lay above or below the hundred year flood line, for their computer models did not cover this particular part of the Trent/Tame river valleys, but their advice was that we ought to assume that we could get flooded. The answer seemed to be either to build a bund or to raise the whole Visitor Centre footprint and proposed car park by about two metres. It would require a massive amount of material to achieve this, with thousands of lorry deliveries and weeks of compaction. Yet again the project was being challenged by what could have been an enormous cost even before any trees were planted. But yet again we had a saviour. Harrington & Son were the company charged with infilling the large holes created through Redland's gravel extraction. They immediately saw a mutual benefit in bringing in more inert material to the site than would otherwise been possible if they had had to stop work once the original ground level had been reached. The Harringtons therefore raised, compacted and landscaped the visitor centre at no cost to the NMA, and by so doing not only saved us some £80,000 but allowed us to place this sum in our matching funding as a gift-in-kind. Without any major financial grant we were beginning to make giant strides towards matching the Millennium Commission award of £1.5 million to pay for our building. Working backwards, we had estimated that this was both the sum needed to establish the planted area and the amount that we could realistically, given our resources, raise in the five years available to us until the Millennium. Therefore, the visitor centre had to be built to the same budget level to ensure we got the funding we required and did not overstretch ourselves. *Architype* thus found themselves working to a fixed budget with a free hand to design a building to fit the amount.

The result was a long, tall, single-storey structure, clad in oak and with a great deal of natural light and ventilation. Some environmentally friendly features, such as a grass roof, did not survive the raised eyebrows of the Trustees or the comments of the planners. Others, such as reed-bed drainage or total recycling of waste and grey water were simply unaffordable, it was obvious that conservation carried its own costs. Nevertheless, the building incorporated many of *Architype*'s ideas and, with its long gallery, large shop, cafeteria and conference room was more than adequate for our initial needs. Only the office space was found wanting but that it was so was a sign of success. Crucially as far as public reaction was concerned, both the kitchen and lavatories could handle all but the largest crowd in a timely fashion – there were to be few queues. Above all the building looked good and right for the site. When, as part of the requirement of the Millennium Commission, we presented the plans to the Royal Fine Art Commission we were told that we would be heard in silence and dismissed without comment. Quite the reverse, the panel Chairman exuded warmth, interest and enthusiasm and made many helpful suggestions. When we were finally able to start building the very fact that a structure was going up on the site added to the project's credibility and helped convince people that we were here to stay. A variety of vicissitudes kept us less convinced, but although the bough on which our cradle swung bent to the limit on several occasions it never broke and we delivered on time and within budget. We were, importantly, also able to involve local people in the fitting out of the building. A part of the shop was set aside for the sale of appropriate crafts produced in the area and when we advertised this we were overwhelmed by the response. Judith Thorpe, who was acting as the quality controller, noticed some water colours that were far superior to any other work. They had been painted by Helen Pilgrim, who lived in a neighbouring farm, and who thenceforward not only displayed her work but organised many art exhibitions in the conference room until motherhood meant that she had to lay aside her paints in favour of crayons.

Designing an arboretum on a site whose boundaries were not finalised and whose funding was not in place was not easy. Added to that was the fact that to be a success the project required numerous partners, some of whom we could identify and approach but others we would know nothing of until they contacted us. The essential players were the three armed Services, but when we began we had no idea in what way they would wish to be involved. I also considered that the spirit in which we were planting required United Nations representation. This was scarcely a detailed planning brief to give a designer but Forest Enterprise were very willing to draw up a proposal for us, and it was their early ideas for the original site on which our future plans would be based.

As was to be expected, Forest Enterprise's speciality and our desire to start with a simple woodland planting meant that our initial drawings were of a sylvan setting. The change of site coincided with the realisation that we needed to involve specialist Landscape Architects and we were lucky to find a company, EDA, whose London Office was ten minutes walk from my own and who also had one of their team, Anthony Darbyshire, based very close to Lichfield. Anthony was an enthusiast; no one thing that he turned his hand to was done without a plethora of ideas spinning off his sketch book. He combined this design enthusiasm with very practical skills and he was not averse to getting himself coated in mud from head to toe when it was necessary, and it was very necessary on the muddy field which we were creating through ripping up the surface to improve the drainage.

Although we were delighted that Redland had generously donated the site neither they nor we would have considered it to be first class agricultural land, nor were we under any illusion that had it been so, or appropriate for any more rewarding land use, we would have secured it. That having been said, Redland, mainly through Ron Foster, had an excellent record of restoring gravel pits and quarries to become wonderful and significant wild life habitats and sanctuaries; our arboretum was for them a different but not an unrelated proposal to create the maximum benefit from an unprepossessing site.

In its original state such flood-plain land might have been reasonably productive agriculturally, but the very act of extracting the gravel brought with it resultant degradation. When the top soil had been bulldozed off to expose the gravel beds beneath it had been piled up in large mounds where twenty years of sun and rain leached out the nutrients leaving just dust and stone, and a remarkable amount of dormant weed seed. Once the gravel was extracted the site became a landfill site into which a lot of rubble and motorway scrapings were dumped. As the tippers deposited their load the resulting piles were bulldozed up and down to compact the debris until sufficient had been unloaded to raise the level to its original height. Then the topsoil was returned. As this operation began at the near end of the pit it meant that every yard of topsoil was being constantly compacted by heavy machinery traversing it many times each day. The result was a badly drained area which, as it was already in the flood plain of the River Tame, could be waterlogged both through winter rains and summer floods either from the river or, more frequently, the sluggish stream that formed the other boundary which, when in flood, used to take a short cut across the site to join the river. Alternatively, in a dry summer, the soil could cake as hard as concrete while any wind from the Redland works coated the leaves of the trees with a fine coating of dust. It was, thus, not an ideal site for planting trees but it was the site that we had and we had to make it a success.

The initial area that we had been given by Redland had been re-grassed some years ago and, when we began work, its coarse grass was being grazed by sheep and horses. Anthony's initial design included an open drain, immediately christened the Darbyshire Ditch, to channel the stream water as it crossed the site and a deep ripping of the whole site to improve the drainage elsewhere. Only once this was done could we think about planting trees, and to begin that work we needed funding well above that which the Appeal had so far brought in. Once more assistance was at hand.

As a part of the package of incentives to encourage landowners in The National Forest to plant trees they could apply, on a competitive basis, for a grant over and above that available for this purpose from the Forestry Commission. We felt confident that our proposals for what could become a major attraction in the area would qualify for an award but, nevertheless, it was an anxious time waiting for the winners to be announced, for without such funding we would have been set back many years and well beyond the Millennium Commission target dates. Michael Heseltine, a great tree man himself, when Secretary of State for the Environment, had initiated the idea of the National Forest and he it was who came to present the award certificates. He came by helicopter and arrived two hours late; our grant, when he announced it, made the wait worthwhile. We now had twelve months to plant our matrix of trees.

However, we were awarded the grant before the paper work for our lease was complete; indeed that simple agreement took over three years to be signed. We could not wait that long to begin work. Both the Millennium Commission and the National Forest needed to see something happening if they were to translate our submission into cash. Yet our Trustees would have been in dereliction of duty if they had approved our starting work before a leasing agreement was in place. On 17 December 1996 David Puttnam wrote me a letter in which he stated that he was 'not at all comfortable with the notion of moving ahead with the speed that you indicate.' Quite rightly he felt that the Trustees needed more legal reassurance than I was in a position to give them. There was every indication that this would take far too long to organise and that we would, in the meantime, lose our grant. Having throughout my naval career never had any opportunity to emulate the actions of Admiral Lord Nelson, nows in retirement came my blind eye moment. Knowing that Redland were not going to renege on their agreement, I ordered the planting to start without informing the Trustees. Redland did not let me down.

The winter of 1996/97 was a very wet one; contractors and volunteers waded knee deep in mud to plant their small saplings in the sodden soil. Every tree of those initial 60,000 also required a rabbit guard so it was tiring and demanding work. In addition, Anthony was determined that his rows would be precise and he did not allow a single plant to be heeled in even a few inches out of line. He had to design this matrix planting to satisfy both the requirements of the grant and our own aspirations. To qualify for the grant we had to plant to a density of 1200 trees to the hectare throughout the site and we were only allowed to leave twenty per cent open land, including avenues, in which we could create plots for our donors. This led to the creation of four large open squares of about an acre each for our early major donors and a large circular area for our United Nations plot. Other donor plots would have to be formed from the matrix planting where the trees could be linked to either individuals or smaller groups.

Given the ground conditions we had very limited choice as to which trees we could plant initially to establish the woodland. They had to be hardy above ground and not mind standing for long periods in water. This meant that the majority of trees planted were Willow (*Salix alba, Salix caprea, Salix cinerea*), Poplar (*Populus tremula, Populus alba, Populus x canescens*) and Alder (*Alnus glutinosa, Alnus incana*). The latter were particularly suitable as the nearby village of Alrewas (impossible to pronounce correctly unless you are a native) means 'the wet area among the alders' while the name 'Lichfield' harks back to 'a clearing among the grey trees'. These three species would grow rapidly and act as nurse trees for the species that we wished to see become established such as oak, both deciduous and evergreen (*Quercus robur, Quercus petraea* and *Quercus ilex*), Cherry (*Prunus avium* and *Prunus padus*) and Scots pine (*Pinus sylvestris*). It was not a great variety but it was selected for one major task and that was to re-establish successfully a Midlands wood on a soggy flood plain. My inexperience led to insufficient wild cherry being planted so that visitors were not to able to share Housman's delight in the Spring when the

> Loveliest of trees, the cherry now
> Is hung with blossom along the bough,
> And stands about the woodland ride
> Wearing white at Eastertide.

Yet even with careful choice we had a large number of failures that first season, with some twelve per cent of the stock dying. We planted replacements with some trepidation but nearly every one of them took. The site could, however, spring unpleasant surprises. One February, in the fourth year of growth, a week of heavy rain was followed by a sudden cold snap with a raw wind blowing from the North. In the morning we found that the majority of evergreen holm oaks, which had done rather well, had been killed; it was as if the wind had passed over the site and laid an icy finger on them and no other tree.

It was always a cold site and until our Visitor Centre was open we did not even have a site office in which to shelter or sit down with potential donors or interested groups. Instead we used to adjourn to the snug in The Crown Inn at Alrewas, a beautiful half-timbered old pub with the most wonderful hanging baskets. The size of the sandwiches, always 'doorstop', and the fact that we seemed to have our own private board room in a pub impressed most visitors, especially any with a service background. When there was a need to provide refreshment on a larger scale, such as after dedicatory planting events, we all crossed over the road to the Alrewas Royal British Legion where we were made welcome by Derek Hopkins, the Chairman, and his wife, Marie, the Secretary and organiser of some excellent lunches. Alrewas was proving to be a most helpful village and it was from here that the initiative to establish a 'Friends' organisation began as one of the clearest and most heartening indications that our project had met with positive local support. Alerted by a newspaper article that we were planning a national arboretum in her parish, the Chairman of Alrewas Parish Council, Carol Davies-Lee, had got in touch to suggest, gently, that it would have been courteous to have informed the locals before the rest of the country. She was right but her main point was that the project would succeed best if local people felt involved and able to contribute. Some already were. From the start, a retired surveyor and Royal Tank Veteran, Sam Kent, had taken upon himself to walk the boundaries of the site both to keep an eye on things and to make a photographic record of developments. Accompanying Sam was another Veteran, Frank Kent, no relation, and the two of them became very early advocates for our cause, to be followed by a rapidly growing number of other individuals. Carol's great idea was to channel all the offers of help that we received into one organisation, 'The Friends of the National Memorial Arboretum' (see Appendix A) ,which would not only provide guides and speakers but also a pool of willing labour to undertake planting and maintenance. Apart from Carol the early members included the already heavily involved Jackie Fisher, the two Kents and Sylvia Kelly, a very skilled flower decorator. From this core of keenness grew a group who manned the site whenever there was an event, running the carpark, catering, ushering and mustering so that I was left to meet and greet our guests and conduct Services or tree planting safe in the knowledge that I need not concern myself with the essential routine arrangements. With Carol's involvement we got another two-for-one-deal, for her husband, Roger, ran a film company that specialised in promotional videos and took on the task of recording all the major events at the site. In fact the Friends became very much a family affair with most members who were married joining as a husband and wife team. This made great sense for the commitments were often at the weekend and thus couples had the opportunity to support us while working together. Their duties included in the first two years, walking the site and looking into each tree guard to note the failures.

It was concern about these losses that had made me decide that no trees would be dedicated to individuals until they were seen to be well established. This could have been planned differently, for the lack of identification caused a great deal of consternation when people arrived, having been told that a tree had been planted in accordance with their wishes, only to be told that it could not, as yet, be identified although we had many thousands of labels printed and ready to go out. What I should have done was to identify saplings in the matrix and list putative dedications on a sheet of paper. In the end, Bob Morris, one of our 'Friends', took upon himself the task of labelling and recording the trees; a mammoth undertaking which could not have been achieved without his dedication.

Every tree dedicated by an organisation and many of those planted in tribute to an individual was planted with a dedicatory plaque beside it. These were made by Blinford Graphics in Walsall, a company we had come across when its founder Ernie Blincow, a Normandy Veteran and member of the 55 Div veterans' association ('Friends of Thierry-Harcourt') had attended the planting of a beech tree brought over to the Arboretum by the mayor of Thierry-Harcourt, the town liberated by 55 Div. Ernie's son Barry willingly tried several designs for plaques and the rod by which they were to be inserted in the ground until we were both content that they had a design that would be easy to insert and would remain in place. Even after that, when we had the paint peel from a large number of the early plaques, Blinford took every one back and redid them to avoid any further failure. But saying that they were designed for easy insertion is to ignore the conditions that a hot summer could create at the site when the ground could assume the consistency of concrete. Inserting any plaques then required arm-aching effort. Nevertheless we had two 'Friends', Ralph Rose and his wife Maureen, who took on this job and spent months placing hundreds of memorial plaques in position.

Although most of the trees in the Arboretum were planted in memory of people who had died, it was never our intention that the site should have the solemnity of a cemetery or that the trees should just be a living version of a tombstone or memorial slab. Rather the whole purpose of the project was to celebrate a life and the contribution those whose names were being recorded here had made not only to those that had known them but to their generation and to the generations that would follow after. It needed to be a joyous site, and the family atmosphere generated by the 'Friends' certainly contributed mightily to this aim.

The site was a living tribute and we wanted those who visited, in the words we often quoted from Isaiah at our Services to:

go out with joy, and be led forth with peace: the mountains and the hills shall break forth before you into singing, and all the trees of the field shall clap their hands.

For our vision was summed up in the verse that follows:

> Instead of the thorn shall come up the fir tree, and instead of the briar shall come up the myrtle tree: and it shall be to the Lord for a name, for an everlasting sign that shall not be cut off.

However, creating woodland where once had been pasture came with a possible downside. In summer one walked across the uncultivated areas to the accompaniment of larks singing in the sky while, often hares would dash away from in front of one's feet. If one was out in the very early morning it was possible to watch a fox on patrol or a pair of little owls in the short grass near the gas pipeline. The Arboretum, on the banks of two great Midlands rivers was also on a wild bird migratory route so the whole area was rich in wildlife. It was important not to lose this diversity although the rabbit population was one we could have done without. Luckily we had in Richard Thorpe, one of the 'Friends', a knowledgeable wildlife expert who wished to share his enthusiasm with others. Richard organised wildlife audits, (see Appendix B), erected bird feeding tables, led nature walks and bat observation evenings and introduced many visitors to the natural world at the NMA. Richard's walks became a major attraction at the site and he planned to erect an 'otter box' on an island in the Tame to encourage those delightful creatures to settle in our stretch of water.

The fact that evidence of travelling otters had been found was itself a tribute to the Environment Agency's work on the River Tame. In my first two summers on the site that river was dank and smelly; over the years it became cleaner and clearer and once more a supporter of fish and river bank creatures. Not only did the Agency improve the water quality but they improved the banks as well. Previously the Tame had flowed through steep, almost canalised sides. Now, thanks to Andrew Crawford at their nearby office, bulldozers contoured the sides and restored the natural look as well as providing shallows in which reeds would grow and provide shelter for many species of water birds. The NMA needed to 'develop' all its amenities and a pleasant river walk was certainly one that it could offer.

Our site ended where the main line railway crossed the river and its flood plain on a tall viaduct. Beyond the viaduct was a small triangle of land enclosed by the railway and the banks of the rivers Tame and Trent. The land had not been worked by Redland but was only accessible through their gravel works and the NMA. Public access, even if it had been possible through the high and thick forest of nettles, was not an option; yet this was a significant point in the nation's river system for not only did it mark the confluence of the Tame, Trent and smaller Mease but it was also very close to the Trent's southernmost reach before it turned again northward towards its junction with the Humber. Very early on we decided that we had to get hold of that most significant 'island' and open it up for our visitors.

Eventually the determination to create pleasant river walks expanded beyond our immediate site and led to the creation of the 'Central Rivers' initiative, which was to examine the best way that the public could benefit from a coordinated use of the land lying in a narrow triangle bounded by Lichfield, Burton upon Trent and Tamworth. In the middle of this space lay our Arboretum, which we felt should form a hub through which cycle- and walkways should pass linking the towns and villages. There were, however, complications as far as our site was concerned. A footpath, fallen into disuse while Redland worked the site, already crossed our site and was starting to be reused. This meant that people could legitimately walk through the Arboretum without paying and, although they should stay on the footpath, there was nothing practical that we could do to ensure that they did not wander elsewhere on the site. Patrols would be confrontational, outside the spirit of the project and expensive on manpower; honesty boxes, probably impractical. Now, while we were still wrestling with this problem, the Central Rivers Board which, along with ourselves included the local council, gravel companies, landowners and the Environment Agency , were welcoming the latter's generous proposal to fund a footbridge across the Trent that would extend that footpath from our site for many more miles, in accordance with the groups, stated objectives, and our often expressed fervent desire. Looked at from our own private, short term interests, this could have led to a flood of non-paying visitors crossing the site just as such a revenue source was becoming vital to our survival: looked at as a member of 'Central Rivers' it was a positive development. We voiced our concerns and signed up. Shortly after the bridge opened we were awarded government grant-in-aid to allow us to open free of charge.

In parallel with our planting, building and maintenance programme we needed to publicise our project to encourage involvement and support. With no publicity budget and a site which was, as yet, not suitable to walk around, the best way to achieve this was to stage a number of events that would encourage media interest. Such an opportunity arose with the celebration of the Golden Wedding Anniversary of the Queen and the Duke of Edinburgh. To mark the occasion we planned to plant a Golden Grove. Like the royal couple, anyone who was celebrating their Golden Wedding in 1997 was a member of a wartime generation and many would have courted in anxious times. What better symbol of joy arising out of the sorrow and sacrifice of war could there be than a plot in tribute to those who had triumphed so obviously over darkness and despair. Again, with the support of John Carey of *The Daily Telegraph* who had given us our first national coverage, we publicised the opportunity to plant celebratory trees. Beverley Fry, a wonderful painter of trees and flowers , provided the paper with some inspiring illustrations which drew forth a swift response and very soon our Golden Grove trees had all been sponsored.

The Golden Grove was formed within a circular mound of earth, representing an iron age circle and symbolising permanency. Within this circle, the garden designer Katherine Swift planned an outer ring of Golden Ash, *Fraxinus excelsior* 'Jaspidea', whose golden stems would provide the relevant colour all year round. Enclosed by the ash trees, which were also an ancient symbol of the life force, were trees whose leaves or berries were, at some stage during the year and coincidentally with the date of the donors' anniversary, also golden. These included, *Sorbus* 'Sunshine', *Sorbus* 'Joseph Rock', *Sorbus* 'Ethel's Gold', and the ornamental apples, *Malus* 'Golden Hornet', 'Wintergold' and *transitoria*. In the centre we planted a circle of golden crocuses. In the autumn of 1999 the Grove was further enhanced when Staffordshire Girl Guides volunteered to plant 10,000 daffodil bulbs on the surrounding bank as their Millennium project. Now every Spring, as the crocuses fade, the golden daffodils toss their heads in sprightly dance.

However, the date of the Queen and Duke's anniversary preceded our planting of the Golden Grove by several months; moreover, the walk to the site was quite a long one and the fine Avenue that we were going to have in place was at the time a long and muddy track. Not that this would have been of vital importance had not the Lord Lieutenant, James Hawley, kindly invited the Duke of Kent to represent the Queen at a celebratory planting to which all Staffordshire couples celebrating their own Golden Wedding in 1997 would be invited. As was becoming customary in these early years we placed the tree, for this occasion a fastigiate Golden Beech, *Fagus sylvatica* 'Dawyck Gold', which the Duke would ceremonially 'plant', temporarily at the top of the site where we had room to erect a huge marquee around it. 'How very, clever', said one gentleman, 'to be able to get a marquee this size around the Queen's tree.' In addition to meeting the Duke, all the couples were to be presented with a slice of the Golden Anniversary cake which he cut and which had been made for the occasion by Graham Hindley, a Stafford baker. The Duke made sure that he met all these special guests although he did ask the first two couples,'And when did you get married?' before realizing that the answer on every occasion would be the same. It had been a simple occasion: a few words, the cutting of a cake, a tree planting and a royal walkabout. At the end many of the couples came over to say that the event had made their celebration something really special. It was moments like that which made us realize how very important our work was to so many. As we had also made use of the occasion to invite Sir David Goodall, Chairman of 'Leonard Cheshire' to plant a similar tree to mark the Golden Jubilee of Leonard's eponymous charity, the event had an added significance for us all.

The Duke of Kent's visit on 21 January 1998 was a major milestone. It came when planting on the site was well underway, but because the arrangements for the day, including the bussing in of so many Staffordshire couples, involved both County and District Councils as well as the Lord Lieutenant, it meant that we had become a part of the accepted local civic scene. We had also given a very special day to people from the generation to whom the Arboretum had been dedicated and been assisted in so doing by the WRVS, another organization whose work was redolent of our aims. Whatever maverick status we might have had we were now 'establishment'. Our saplings had a future.

CHAPTER TWO

Divinity and Douglas Firs: The Millennium Chapel of Peace and Forgiveness

Thou art in Trees -
Thy Strength
Thy Beauty
Service,
All in Trees...

Thus Thou art known,
Art felt,
Art seen,
Thou art in Trees

Nancy Price

The young man looked around as he walked in and then beckoned to his parents to follow him. He led them over to the altar and, seeing a volunteer watching him, asked permission to lift up the altar cloth. When he had done so he placed a finger on the words engraved across the wood at the top and read them out:

When I was in prison ye visited me

'I done that', he said. He moved to the back of the altar and read again:

Thy Father that seest in secret will reward thee openly

'And that,' he said. Although the pride in his voice was very evident some three years had passed between the time he had helped carve those words and his first showing them to his parents. This had been unavoidable. He had been inside Swinfen Hall Young Offenders Institute when he had been asked to do the work and had only recently been released.

The young men at Swinfen Hall had played a major part in furnishing the Chapel at the Arboretum for it was they who had made the altar, lectern and pulpit and moved closer to an HND certificate by so doing. Their involvement had been considered crucial for the development of not only the Chapel but the spirit of the site as well. The Arboretum, although centred upon Remembrance, could only succeed if it had a message for the future and a message which would appeal to the young. Very early on this belief that the project was a bridge between the past and the future was summed up in the slogan:

'Remember the Future'

Unless youngsters could have a role in the creation of the Arboretum then its future could not be guaranteed nor its message listened to; for this to happen the lads at Swinfen Hall had as important a part to play as the Veterans' organizations. Involving local youth did, of course, also provide an insurance against any vandalism; none was ever noticed.

So school children both locally and nationally became involved. At a local level they attended and took part in both tree planting and Armistice Day Services where Repton School Combined Cadet Force, Sutton Coldfield Sea Cadets and Lichfield Grammar provided a guard, an orchestra and a bugler, while local primary school children added the joy and excitement of youth.

As the Millennium approached, Andrew Lloyd Webber, became concerned that the nation was forgetting what event was being celebrated, and to remind people he launched a competition to write a Millennium Prayer. The winner was a thirteen year old school girl from the Royal Hospital School, Holbrook, and Lord Lloyd Webber then paid to have Anna Crompton's prayer carved and mounted at the entrance to the Millennium Chapel. I had asked that the prayer be carved on cedar wood and after it was in position proudly announced this fact to gathered congregations, only to be told, quietly, by one of the woodcarvers that it was in fact cherry. Whatever the material, the words spoke eloquently to many visitors:

> Dear Lord our heavenly father,
> at the dawn of a new millennium,
> in a world of darkness,
> give us your light;
> In lands of war and prejudice,
> grant us peace;
> In a world of despair,

give us hope;
In a world of sadness and tears,
show us your joy;
In a world of hatred,
show us your love;
In a world of arrogance,
give us humility;
In a world of disbelief,
give us faith.
Give us courage to face the challenges
of feeding the hungry, clothing the naked,
housing the homeless and healing the sick.
Give us the power to make a difference in your world,
and to protect your creation.
Through Jesus Christ, Our Lord,
Amen

Children also featured in the major work inside the Chapel. When the Essex woodcarvers, who created the 49 Division Polar Bear memorial, found out that there was to be a Chapel on the site they volunteered to carve something for the inside. The choice of subject was left to them and, being who they were, they delivered two works. The first was a copy of the processional cross at Walsingham, a favourite place of pilgrimage for Baroness Sue Ryder, the founder of the eponymous homes and services, who was married to Leonard Cheshire and a Trustee of the Arboretum.

Their second piece of work was 'The Storyteller.' The Chapel was designed to be supported by twelve wooden pillars, one for each of the apostles. These were made from Douglas Fir, *Pseudotsuga menziesii*, chosen to mark the coincident two hundredth anniversary of the birth of David Douglas, the great plant explorer who had first introduced the species to this country from the Pacific north-west of America. It was then felt that each of the pillars should depict one of the twelve apostles. Originally these portraits were going to be carved into the pillars themselves but concerns about the strength of the structure, later remedied, meant that the carvings had to be created separately and then affixed. They were made by a Shropshire woodcarver and ex-Royal Marine, Jim Heath, who depicted both the saint's face and the symbols associated with him. Thus, Saint Peter, outside the door, held in his hands the keys while at his feet there was a crowing cockerel; Saint Andrew had his saltire, Saint James his scallop shell while Saint Matthew's form was based on the tax man who features on so much Inland Revenue literature, allowing the virtue of humour to be reflected in the Chapel. The 'rock' on which Saint Peter stood we made from a number of different stones symbolizing the fact that after two thousand years the Church remains disunited. The woodcarvers saw these Saints as a way of linking the past with the future. Their gift would be a carving showing a Christ-like figure, based on their local parish priest, sitting at the bottom of a flight of stairs and telling a story familiar to the disciples on the pillars to a group of twelve young children. What made the carving extra special was that each child was carved from studies of the woodcarvers' grandchildren and those children were able to attend both the dedication of the Chapel and the Queen's visit. 'The Storyteller' immediately became a favourite with the public, and few other objects on the site provide such a palpable link with the future.

The size of the Chapel had to be defined by the budget available. For a while we flirted with the idea of launching a separate appeal for this building, before deciding that we should keep our hand firmly on the plough and our eye along the one furrow we were already working. The funds would have to be a part of the general appeal. It would not need to be a large building as most users would be groups of less than a hundred, frequently just small family groups wanting to gather in the Chapel as part of a commemorative tree planting – they would not want to be intimidated by a large structure, besides which, if we got the design right we would be able to use the area outside as part of the Chapel for major services. We therefore agreed that we should plan on a building that should seat one hundred and in an area that would be sufficiently light and open to make it feel part of the Arboretum, not a gloomy, private and possibly unwelcoming space for those not used to being inside a place of worship.

And a place of worship and reflection we wanted it to be rather than a spot linked firmly to one religion. We wanted Christians, Muslims, Jews, Hindus, Buddhists, Zoroastrians, those of any faith or none to feel comfortable within its walls and comforted by its ambience. However, early discussions with various faith groups left us with the very firm message that if we tried to please them all we would end up pleasing none of them. Rather, we should clearly reflect a Christian tradition but emphasize the inclusivity and welcoming nature of the best traditions in our own communion. This meant, in my view, that many of the fittings would tell a subliminal story to those who had been brought up as Christians but would be understandable and inoffensive to others. 'The Storyteller' was a good example, representing as it did a man of faith recounting tales to a group of youngsters; given the setting, the viewer could conclude that the message that he was proclaiming was one of peace and harmony.

Although the building was designated 'The Millennium Chapel' and was to be the only place of worship built in the country to celebrate that anniversary, it also needed a dedicatory name. Our desire that the building be one in which people of any faith or none might feel at home precluded naming it for a Saint, even that of the much loved local one, Saint Chad even the millennially appropriate Christ's Chapel seemed not quite right and also, for our small endeavour, somewhat presumptuous. Far away in South Africa and closer to home in Northern Ireland millennium lamps of hope were being lit with the idea of 'Peace and Reconciliation'; old enemies and hostile cultures were trying to acknowledge their wickedness one to the other, to embrace each other and endeavour to live in harmony while accepting that they had different cultures and traditions. The strong, positive, hopeful message of the millennium was that a new age was beginning in celebration of the anniversary of the coming of the Prince of Peace, and it was that message of the virtues of peace and its fellow traveller reconciliation that we were trying to make the redolent atmosphere of the site: 'Peace and Reconciliation' for which we were being given the marvellous example of the actions and words of Nelson Mandela and Archbishop Desmond Tutu. Yet on reflection 'reconciliation' seemed too passive a word; after all one can become reconciled without a major change in outlook or a growth of love to replace hate, but one has to take a positive step to 'forgive'. The Chapel thus became 'The Millennium Chapel of Peace and Forgiveness.'

The concept of 'forgiveness' was displayed graphically behind the altar where three crosses were hung from the wall. The central cross was the very recognizable 'sword of sacrifice' that is a feature on plinths at all major Commonwealth War Graves Cemeteries. It was flanked by two rough crosses roped together from branches of dead elms from my garden roped. From these hung four handcuffs, presented by the West Midland Serious Crime Group. On one of these crosses the handcuffs are both open, signifying forgiveness; on the other one is open and the other still shut – a symbol of eventual forgiveness for all. However, visitors did occasionally reach up and snap shut the open pair of handcuffs, one gentleman doing so with his son's hand inside, necessitating a rather embarrassing call to the local police station for help to release him. In the eleven short verses from Luke's Gospel account of the crucifixion, on which our display was based, the key words are 'forgive' and 'remember', the major purpose of the whole Arboretum. Below the crosses we wrote the words that conclude a G K Chesterton hymn, 'O God of earth and altar':

> Raise up a living nation,
> A single sword to thee.

This was germane to our desire that the Arboretum should be a focus for the whole nation as a symbol of peace, remembrance, service, reconciliation and forgiveness.

In front of the crosses stood the altar for which we were presented a cross made from burr oak by a young apprentice cabinet maker whose grandmother, Barbara Roberts, was a leading light in the George Cross Island Association; yet again, one contact had led to another in an entirely different direction. The Arboretum throve on such links.

Either side of the altar cross were placed two candle sticks. Lichfield is the home of the renowned cutlery makers Arthur Price of England who had just produced a celebratory 'Millennium Dawn' range. The company were most willing to donate twelve of the knives from this set to be formed into two candlesticks. The thinking behind this was that if one viewed the altar as representing the table at which the Last Supper was held, then each disciple was bound to have had a knife. Placed upright in a circle they could symbolize the need for both earthly and heavenly bread, and when we linked them with a silver barbed wire we showed that people were still unable to share such bread because of man's inhumanity to man. The subliminal reference to the symbol of Amnesty International was also deliberate. We took the knives and the idea down to Robert Pritchard-Gordon, a Lichfield silversmith, and he translated these into a striking design sponsored by the Lichfield jeweller, Robert Carr.

The final addition to the altar was probably the most telling as it linked youth with a past wartime generation. We were visited by a students from the Lamarck School at Albert on the Somme. Their school had been named after the local botanist Albert Lamarck who had brought back the superb red-leafed, white-flowered shrub, *Amelanchier lamarckii*, from North America, and the school wished to plant a specimen at the Arboretum. In preparation for their journey they had wandered through the World War One trenches outside their town and gathered up shrapnel, which they had melted down and shaped into a bas-relief picture of Christ. It was a most appropriate gift for our Chapel of Peace.

That gift brought to mind the sufferings of individuals in war and conflict; but we also wanted the Chapel to be a focus for remembrance in a national sense. For too many of us the idea of remembrance conjures up a visions of old men marching past the Cenotaph on Remembrance Sunday. Yet remembrance is something that should be present every day of our lives as the Far East Prisoners' of War Association emphasize in their refrain:

> And we that are left grow old with the years,
> Remembering the heartache, the pain and the tears,
> Hoping and praying that never again,
> Man will sink to such sorrow and shame.
> The price that was paid we will always remember
> Every day , every month, not just in November.

I wanted the Arboretum to deliver this daily reminder, perhaps, at the symbolic hour of 11 o'clock in the morning when there would be visitors around to join in.

The layout of The Chapel suggested the idea of designing the building so that, at eleven o'clock every morning a shaft of sunlight struck the altar. This could then be linked to the observation of a two-minute silence every day at this time. A line of windows high on the Chapel's wall meant that the sun's rays would be present, but we fitted a spotlight to cheat when it was cloudy. The next challenge was indicating the observance of the silence. It seemed logical to introduce it with the playing of 'Last Post' and conclude it with 'Reveille' but, given the location of the site these would have to be taped. Charles Lewis, the Director of Corporate Affairs at The Royal British Legion and an NMA enthusiast, organized the Band of the Royal Marines to provide the recording that we needed. Charles went further and arranged for the BBC newsreader Peter Donaldson to tape an introduction to the Silence by telling the story of its origins, while in the background the Royal Marines played 'Nimrod' and other music familiar to all who have listened to the Remembrance Sunday ceremony at the Cenotaph. Putting light and broadcast together so that they would come on just before the Silence which would start at precisely 11 o'clock every day of the year was a complicated challenge which was successfully undertaken by Roger Davies-Lee, who was a communications specialist and film maker who also videoed all our major events.

Charles Lewis and I were also able to work together on an idea that was dear to his heart – the reintroduction of the Silence at 11.00 am on 11 November, the time that the guns fell silent at the end of the First World War and the occasion when it had been commemorated until the decision was made to move the event to the nearest Sunday to 11 November. We had decided that we would hold an Armistice Day Service from the moment we moved on to the site. This meant, in the first years, strimming a path across the fields and clearing sufficient space to accommodate the Lord Lieutenant, James Hawley, his wife, Susan, and other dignitaries and guests. Standing there in a windswept (but luckily rain-free) field, surrounded by rough pasture, they must have wondered whether anything was going to come of this idea. But they came back each year and the event grew with tents and then marquees until we were able, at last, to move in to the Chapel itself. All this time James and Susan Hawley remained enthusiastic advocates as did The Royal British Legion, whose Women's Section always sent a strong delegation to attend our Armistice Day Services. Perhaps any doubts these guests had as to our ability to deliver were eased by the fact that from the beginning both BBC and ITN broadcast the Last Post, nationwide, from the site at 11.00 am on the 11

November. One year the producer expressed grave concern that the bugler, from Repton School, who was just five foot four and aged fourteen, would not be man enough for the task; a quick rehearsal assured him that the necessary talent was alive and relaxed in that small form. As the occasion grew in importance so we invited various groups to plant trees as part of the ceremony. Initially these trees had to be planted in a holding area until their final location was ready to receive them. Sadly, some were lost in the interval, but all were replaced.

After one of her visits, Mary Arnold, President of the Women's Section of TRBL offered to provide an altar frontal for the Chapel and, in so doing, established another major theme for the Chapel and the Arboretum itself. With Mary I visited a small business specializing in stitching church furnishings to discuss the design for the altar cloth. One idea leapt out at us – the tree of life. Based on Revelations 22 verse 2:

> In the midst of the street of it, and on either side of the river, was there the tree of life, which bare twelve manner of fruits, and yieldeth her fruit every month; and the leaves of the tree were for the healing of the nations.

This would form a symbol of our hopes and incorporate the spirit in which we wished to plant our trees. Later, the Right Revd John Bickersteth, seeing the altar frontal, presented the Chapel with a tree of life banner which had been made for him by the ladies of Wells Cathedral when he had been the Bishop of Bath and Wells.

The commissioning of the altar frontal made us consider how best to create drops for both the pulpit and the lectern. The Trefoil Guild, for whom we were designing a plot, suggested that one of their number, Enid Newman, would love to undertake the work as long as we provided her with a design. I carefully drew two, based on a globe and a collection of oak leaves from around the world. On one would appear the words from Revelations but on the other, 'And Nation Shall Speak Peace Unto Nation', the motto of the BBC. Apart from the words, little of my original design appeared in the finished articles, which were far superior in every way to those that I had drawn.

There were other ways of involving individuals in the creation of the Chapel's furnishings. Providing the seats and working the kneelers were two such opportunities. For seating we turned to an excellent firm in Bradford who agreed to produce two types of chair, both of which had the millennium year 2000 engraved on them. Every chair was offered up for sponsorship and it was not long before each one was adopted with their dedication noted on small brass plaques which were, some years later, to be the subject of a VAT investigation!

We had wanted to have 100 different designs for the kneelers but the cost of doing this seemed prohibitive, so we produced ten types based on trees either linked to the bible and the Christian story or ones that would be growing in the Arboretum. These included holly and ivy, olive, palm, horse chestnut, autumn leaves and plane. Once again *The Daily Telegraph* acted as our channel to invite people to dedicate seats or work kneelers. The take-up was immediate and within months carefully wrapped kneelers, with dedicatory labels attached, were being delivered to my house and filling up the spare bedroom. We had intended that the seats should be grouped in an arc around the altar rather than be set out in static lines, but the continuing requests to dedicate chairs meant that we increased the number and had to dismiss the idea of stacking most of them until they were needed because visitors would always want to see their own chair in place. In fact the grouping of the seats itself lent the intimacy to the Chapel which we had always wished to achieve.

Apart from a small vestry, the Chapel was a single room of classic proportions. We had wanted something redolent of the places of worship two thousand years ago where the Christian message would have been heard for the first time, and *Architype* had submitted a slab-sided, double cube with a pillared external porch, the proportions of which recalled those of a Greek Temple. Darkening into the sunset the outline of the building gives a feeling of peace, order and continuity that relaxes the eye of the viewer; it was a masterful concept. Unromantically, it was built as a large box balanced on twelve wooden pillars which, Derek Langley found by scrambling onto the roof, were not linked so that when the wind blew the structure swayed alarmingly. Reinforcements had to be built into the walls and the outside pillars braced. The costs for this additional work, and where the responsibility for the defective design lay, were one of the few serious areas of contention between us and the architects. Perhaps more important than any differences, was the fact that the building was completed on time, allowing us sufficient time to introduce the fittings and fixtures ahead of the day set for its dedication, Thursday 2 November 2000. Just before the Service began I received a telephone call from Sue Ryder's secretary to let me know that Lady Ryder, the founder of the eponymous homes and one of our Trustees who had hoped to be with us, had died during the night; our first silence in the completed Chapel was a tribute to her.

The Service was designed around the dedicatory themes of peace and forgiveness and the Order of Service was encompassed by Peace. Thus the first words of the Bishop of Lichfield as he entered The Chapel at the beginning of the Service were:

Peace be to this house and all who enter here.

The Service closed with the Hymn 'Love divine, all love excelling' in which we had amended the final word so that we completed the dedication with the phrase:

> Till we cast our crowns before thee,
> Lost in wonder, love and *peace*.

In between the words of peace the Bishop, having blessed the whole building, eased his way through the crowded congregation to bless with Holy Water the font, lectern, altar, and pulpit. He could not get close enough to the font to see it because of the crowd and had to ask, *sotto voce*, 'Am I aiming in the right direction?' He was. The Service also included the singing of Anna Crompton's Millennium Prayer by her school choir conducted by her father, Peter Crompton.

The Bishop left, to a great peal of bells from the Lichfield Diocesan Mobile Belfry whose enthusiastic presence made up for our not having a peal of our own, leaving us with our first chance to see the reaction of the public to this rather special place. Even leaving aside the delight with Sylvia Kelly's flower decorations, the response was most positive and it has been so ever since. To few is given the opportunity to design a Chapel with their own ideas; the joy of being able so to do and in a way that serves a need and provides a pleasure is a wonderful reward.

Several year later we were asked to arrange for a service in tribute to Lord Farnham who, although not directly involved with the NMA, had been linked to us through his Presidency of both the Freemasons and the International Tree Foundation, both of whom had dedicated plots. Holding a meaningful memorial service to someone about whom, despite his links we did not know much, was going to be difficult, so we wrote a hymn especially for the occasion:

> As the beech within the wood,
> As the pine upon the shore
> As the redwood in the forest
> Rises from the shady floor,
> Lord of life, please help us be
> Strong and upright as a tree.
>
> As the hazel in the hedges
> As the hawthorn and the sloe
> Give shelter to the shorn lamb
> When the icy wet winds blow,
> Lord of caring help us be
> A source of comfort like a tree.

As the orchard's golden fruits
As the orange and the pear
Lime and lemon, nut and sap
Feed thy people everywhere,
Lord of bounty help us be
Full of succour as a tree.

As the blossom of the cherry
And the acer's autumn glow
As the aspen and the willow
When they whiten, row on row,
Lord of beauty let us be
Joy to all just like a tree.

As the dead tree on the hill
Into which the nails were driven
Turned a symbol of despair
To a sign of being forgiven,
Lord of love, please help us be
A sign of love, just like that tree.

By the time of the Service we still did not have an accompanying tune so we recited the words like a psalm. Later we adopted the tune 'England's Lanes' by Geoffrey Shaw which usually accompanies the hymn, 'For the beauty of the Earth'.

The planning for Lord Farnham's Service led to research into services linked with trees and the discovery that following the first world war a project had been launched to link tree planting with Armistice Day. The first planting and service associated with it was held at the Home for Crippled Children at Chailey in Surrey, at which these lines from the poem 'Planting a Tree' by Lucy Larcom were read :

He who plants a tree
He plants love,
Tents of coolness spreading out above;
Wayfarers he may not live to see;
Gifts that grow our best;
Hands that bless are blest.
Plant! Life does the rest.

Armed with this and with the support of the Tree Council we endeavoured to reintroduce a National Tree Sunday but, sadly, although services designed along the lines we drafted were held, (see Appendix C) in a number of churches and at outdoor venues, the idea failed to spark. Perhaps, one day!

Although the Chapel was full of symbolism it was too small to contain all the element that we wished to include. In particular, it was here that I wanted visitors to be reminded of the inspiration behind the whole project – the life and work of Leonard Cheshire. Thus, in front of the Chapel we created an amphitheatre named for Leonard. This was based not upon the Roman idea of a place of bloody slaughter but on the meeting places that the persecuted Huguenots had created in hidden places in the wooded wilderness of the Cevennes. Along the narrow ridge of the amphitheatre bank I invited individual Cheshire Homes to have beech trees planted to form a windbreak. This was a failure. Whatever we did to encourage growth, the saplings shrivelled up and died.

When Leonard Cheshire founded the World Memorial Fund for Disaster Relief he did so in shocked response to the number of lives lost in the conflicts of the twentieth century. To keep his kernel of an idea alive, at the site across the path from the amphitheatre, we built a low circular brick wall in front of which we placed a sign with the following words:

THE WORLD MEMORIAL CAIRN

Over 80,000,000 lives were lost in the wars and conflicts of the
twentieth century which afflicted or affected every nation upon earth.
Some of those who died are remembered within this
Arboretum; the names of many are recorded elsewhere;
a countless number lie forgotten in unmarked graves
or on the ocean bed.

This Cairn pays tribute to them all

Any man's death diminishes me, because I am involved in
Mankind; and therefore never send to know for whom the bell
toll; it tolls for thee

John Donne

We would ask you, the visitor, to pick up a stone
as you walk around and to place it at this site.
As you do so, perhaps, you might pause to reflect upon one,
or a few, or the many, known or unknown to you, who have died and,
reflecting on their fate, say a small prayer for peace.

*For, behold, I create new heavens and a new earth; and the
former shall not be remembered nor come into mind…the wolf
and the lamb shall feed together and the lion shall eat straw like
the bullock; and the dust shall be the serpent's meat. They shall
not hurt or destroy in all my holy mountain, saith the Lord.*

Isaiah 65, vv 17 / 25

Below the writing we placed the picture of a large poppy.

The concept of a memorial cairn was expanded exponentially by the local newspaper which created a mountain out of a molehill with the front page headline:

Eighty Million Rocks will Dominate Alrewas Landscape.

Luckily the paper's concept was never realised, leaving the later Armed Forces Memorial tumulus to be the sole vertical feature on the site.

The Chapel attracted to its vicinity organisations who felt a link to both the church and the military such as the Church Lads' and Church Girls' Brigade and TOC H. The involvement of the former began through one of the early volunteers, Maynard Scott, whose particular pleasure was to give talks about the Chapel either at the site or to groups in the surrounding towns and villages. Maynard had strong links with the Church Lads and Church Girls and spent sometime discussing how those organisations might best be represented at the site. In the end we decided on an open air extension to the Chapel in the form of a rectangular plot with crossed pathways beside which would be planted 22 purple shrubs, *Berberis thunbergii* 'Atropurpurea Nana', each shrub representing one of the Victoria Crosses won by members of the Brigade. When completed it became one of the quiet reflective places in the Arboretum and a tribute not only to the Brigade but to Maynard's essentially individual efforts.

Down the slope from the Brigade's tribute, and across Millennium Avenue, stands a brick plinth surmounted by a large oil lamp – a tribute to the life and work of the Reverend Philip 'Tubby' Clayton and TOC H, the organisation which he began in 1915 in Talbot House at Poperinge in Belgium, just behind the front line to provide a place of rest and sanctuary for British troops. The lamp, the symbol of TOC H, was soon a symbol of compassion and companionship, in the Christian tradition, around the world. One of the first visitors to Talbot House wrote:

To conquer hate would be to end the strife of all the ages, but for men to know one another is not difficult and it is half the battle.

This was a succinct summary of the spirit behind the creation of our Chapel of Peace and Forgiveness.

CHAPTER THREE

The Oak and the Ash and the Bonny Silver Birch: The Armed and Merchant Services

Through God's good grace, through strength of English oak,
We have preserved our faith, our throne, our land;
Now, with our freedom saved from tyrant's yoke,
We plant these trees, Remember why they stand!

Kenyon Gower

*Lines chosen by King George VI for a plaque to be placed
at the Oak Tree Cross in Windsor Great Park*

The *Glasgow Daily Herald* was being bombarded by rocks, but from well-wishers. A week earlier it had run an article bringing readers' attention to the desire to build a cairn at the National Memorial Arboretum with each rock coming from the side of one of the Lochs after which the Loch Class frigates had been named. The full number, and more, arrived within a few days! They were then moved to block up the drive of Ronald Blanchard, of the 'Loch' *Class* Frigates Association, who had to remain trapped indoors until transport was arranged to move them to the NMA to be built into a Scottish cairn, one of the many innovative ways in which Service Associations chose to pay tribute to their colleagues.

The individual Services themselves responded in a variety of ways to the suggestion by their Senior Personnel Officers that units might wish to have a commemorative tree planted at the NMA. The Adjutant General, Sir David Ramsbotham, wrote to all Regiments suggesting that they might like a tree planted in the proposed Army Grove and that a donation of £300 per Regiment might be appropriate. There was no need to look at the amount when the cheques started to arrive; they were all for £300! Every Regiment and Corps in the British Army responded – apart from the Scottish Regiments whose Colonels stated that the proposal was 'too English'. However, after a letter to them suggesting that a sign would be erected stating that a space had been reserved for them at this national site, for when and if they wanted to join in, they relented and had an impressive line of Scots Pine planted. Few serving units of the Royal Navy responded to the appeal but a great number of 'old ships' associations did so, certainly sufficient to plant 'The Review' of oak trees. The RAF responded in equal numbers of existing Air Stations and Squadron Associations. Thus each service became involved in what was to be the central focus of the NMA.

One of the problems we had at the NMA was how to make a plantation of small trees interesting enough to attract visitors during their early years of growth. The answer lay in indicating the importance of what they represented and the stories that lay behind them. By having Ships, Regiments and Squadrons involved we could produce colourful plaques bearing their individual badges, which would provide an interest in even the most insignificant sapling. Thus, well before a tree had grown in stature and established its character, it was identifiable with a unit and the people who served in it. And with the units came the tales. Thus trees were dedicated by survivors of HMS *Glowworm*, which sank after ramming the German cruiser *Hipper*, earning for her Commanding Officer, Lieutenant Commander Gerard Roope, a posthumous Victoria Cross, which his son proudly brought along to the dedication planting. The survivors of Captain Louis Mountbatten's ship, HMS *Kelly*, which was sunk during the evacuation of Crete, were delighted to be joined by their President, the Prince of Wales, for their tree planting and to regale the crowd with tales of Lord Louis. When the Prince came to sign the visitors' book he found the pen scratchy and asked for another. With none immediately available, Sir Henry Every, who had medical connections, reached into his inside pocket and withdrew a biro on which clearly written was the word 'Viagra'. He handed it to Lady Mountbatten, the Prince's godmother who was standing next to him, and she made a comment before passing it to the Prince. 'Hmm!' he said, 'good name for a warship that, HMS *Viagra*'.

Many ex-navy associations were formed around a class of ship or an arm of the Service rather than an individual ship itself. The first to become involved with the project was the First Destroyer Association whose 'Hunt' Class vessels had been the workhorses of the Royal Navy throughout the Second World War and included HMS *Aldenham*, whose loss to a mine off the Dalmatian coast on 14 December 1944 made her the last royal naval vessel sunk by enemy action in the second world war. Many readers and cinema-goers have delighted in the story recounted in *Captain Corelli's Mandolin*, but while this fictional account of German troops replacing Italian ones on the Greek Islands was unfolding, real life drama for a similar reason was taking place on the other side of Greece where Churchill had ordered British troops to seize the Dodecanese Islands in the wake of the Italian surrender. Unfortunately, the Germans reacted faster and by the time the British had despatched their forces the former were in control of the key island of Rhodes with its airfields, leaving the British isolated on Kos and Leros. Not only isolated but without air cover, the troops could only be supplied at night by destroyers moving at full speed through the narrow channels off the Turkish coast so that they could arrive, discharge their cargo and be clear under cover of darkness. Many years later I sailed the same route in a yacht, and even at a sedate four knots we had to be constantly aware of our position so as to avoid grounding. We were very grateful for the frequent lighthouse beams sweeping across the dark sea. With every such light extinguished, the navigating officers of the destroyers who raced through each night displayed extreme professional competence. Many of the ships involved were Hunt Class destroyers of which *Adrias*, a Greek destroyer, formerly HMS *Border*, was one. On the night of 10 September 1943 while making the passage in company with three other similar vessels she struck a mine which blew off her bow. HMS *Hurworth*, going to her rescue, struck another mine and blew up with the loss of 143 men. On board Adrias twenty-one men had been killed and her Captain, Ioannis Toumbas, knocked unconscious. When he came to he found the Coxswain slapping his face and recorded in his report of proceedings, 'He seemed to be enjoying this too much so I told him to stop'. What followed was an act of seamanship that ranks amongst the greatest ever undertaken. With consummate skill Captain Toumbas beached his ship on the Turkish coat to effect repairs and then sailed the bowless *Adrias* over 400 miles back to Alexandria. When the ship eventually crept into harbour the crew of all the other vessels cleared lower decks and cheered her in. A similar welcome had been given to the ship supporting the all but sinking Texaco tanker *Ohio* when, supported by three naval destroyers and having survived days and nights of constant attack, she brought the fuel that the besieged Island of Malta needed to keep its defiant fight against the Axis powers alive. The story of Operation Pedestal, the convoy of which Ohio was the most important, is another great tale of the sea. To many the fictional account of Ulysses wandering around the Mediterranean is the greatest story about sailors in those waters. The real life exploits of the heroes of *Adrias* and Operation Pedestal easily match these stories in the Odyssey and have the advantage of being true. If the NMA keeps them alive and encourages visitors to read about them then it will have served one of its major purposes.

Some of these great tales did, of course, achieve a wide audience when they were made into films such as *The Battle of the River Plate* and *The Yangtze Incident*, which told the story of the escape from under Chinese Communist guns of HMS *Amethyst*. At the NMA, *Amethyst* and the three ship that were supporting her from downstream, HM Ships *Black Swan*, *Consort* and *London* are remembered in a small grove that includes two Chinese Maidenhair trees, *Gingko biloba*, as well as an encircling hedge of 46 shrubs, one for each of the sailors that lost their lives.

One of the most numerous classes of ship ever built was one with the smallest size of vessel, the 'Ton' Class minesweepers of which 118 were constructed of wood and were to serve around the globe for many year in a number of roles. Sadly, it was one of the Ton Class, HMS *Fittleton*, which was to be involved in one of the navy's worst recent peacetime tragedies, when twelve of her company were lost in a collision while undertaking a Replenishment at Sea on 20 September 1976. In tribute to the crew of HMS *Fittleton* and all who had served in minesweepers a plinth and tree were planted at the edge of the Naval Review.

Wartime tragedies were, of course, often far greater. When HMS *Neptune* struck a mine off the coast of Libya on 19 December 1941 she sank with all but one of her crew of 764. HMS *Dunedin* was torpedoed on passage to South Africa and, although seventy-two of her crew survived exposure, thirst, hunger and the baking sun, they left behind another 491 shipmates. Another U-boat casualty was HMS *Royal Oak*, sunk at her anchorage in Scapa Flow on 14 October 1939 with the war scarcely underway. It is memorials such as these that bring to mind Rudyard Kipling's words:

> We have fed our seas for a thousand years
> And she calls us, still unfed,
> Though there's never a wave of all her waves
> But marks our English dead:
> We have strawed our best to the wave's unrest,
> To the shark and the sheering gull.
> If blood be the price of admiralty,
> Lord God, we ha' paid in full!

The Naval Review does more beside. The lost men of ships such as *Neptune, Dunedin, Royal Oak* have no grave but the seabed; in paying tribute to them on British soil the NMA contributes to their souls' return to the land which they loved. On every occasion that a naval tree is planted and dedicated the naval prayer is recited and, although we are far inland, our voices are carried on the wind to float across those waves below which, far more hidden than the rich dust concealed in Rupert Brooke's foreign field, lie the sea-changed bones of our sailors. Read aloud from the pages of this book, it undertakes a similar voyage:

O, Eternal Lord God, who alone spreadest out the heavens and rulest the raging of the sea; who hast compassed the waters with bounds until day and night come to an end: be pleased to receive into thy almighty and most gracious protection the persons of us thy servants and the Fleet in which we served. Preserve them from the dangers of the sea and of the air and from the violence of the enemy; that they may be a safeguard unto our most gracious Sovereign Lady, Queen Elizabeth, and her dominions, and a security for such as pass on the seas upon their lawful occasions; that the inhabitants of our Island and Commonwealth may in peace and quietness serve thee our God; and that they may return in safety to enjoy the blessings of this land, with the fruits of their labours and with a thankful remembrance of thy mercies to praise and glorify thy holy Name; through Jesus Christ our Lord.

Amen

Close to the Ton Class plinth a plot was laid out for the Fleet Air Arm in the shape of that most graceful of sea birds, the gannet, whose folding wings, a split second before the bird plunges into the water, are a delight to witness. This characteristic gave the bird's name to the far less elegant naval aircraft whose wings had to be similarly folded to stow the aircraft below decks on an aircraft carrier.

One year the Arboretum was visited by a retired Norwegian naval officer, Finn-Christian Stumoen, who had spent the war years operating out of Scotland, landing and picking up saboteurs and resistance workers during the dark days of German occupation. Back in the security of their English ports the Norwegians partied and impressed the local girls with their tall good looks and daring deeds. Many, like Finn, married British girls. Even had he not, he retained a love of the country that had given him shelter and a base from which to strike back at his nation's enemy so, after he visited the Arboretum, he was determined that the battle fought by the Norwegians should also be remembered here. On his return to Norway he raised a number of silver birches on his farm and brought them back to the NMA to be planted, with each tree representing one of the thirty ships of the Royal Norwegian Navy lost in the Second World War – a massive number, for every fourth man in that force was killed in the war. When the trees arrived they were the smallest saplings that we had ever planted at the site but they transplanted well and form a graceful Avenue along the boundary of the Arboretum.

For that hybrid group, The Royal Marines, whose motto *Per Mare, per Terram* indicates their ubiquity, and for their wartime comrades, the Army Commandos, it was felt appropriate to plant Alders, trees that do not mind getting their 'feet' wet. A small collection of these trees was donated by Hillier's Arboretum in Hampshire, yet another organisation which was most willing to provide support and guidance to our sapling selves.

Many of the Royal Navy's duties in the second world war had involved escorting merchant ships, and it did seem logical that a tribute of sorts should be included to the crews of those merchant vessels who struggled against great odds to keep our nation, our allies such as Russia and islands such as Malta, supplied with food and other vital resources. It was these merchant sailors who fought the war's longest battle, beginning with the loss of the SS *Athenia* on 3 September 1939 and ending with the sinking of the *Avondale Park* on 7 May 1945, just two of some 2,535 British-flagged merchant ships that were lost through enemy action in the days between. On the floor of every ocean of the world there lie the rusting hulls of these vessels and the bones of some 42,000 seamen who braved the perils of the sea and the violence of the enemy in ships whose life rafts were not fit for purpose, to bring the food and fuel that Britain needed. Theirs was an unglamorous task and their battle was fought well beyond the eye of the cameraman or the pen of the reporter. Those who went down to the sea in ships and occupied their business in great waters did so in the knowledge that between slipping out of harbour and securing alongside no moment was safe from attack. Those on the Malta Convoy or coming into London or Liverpool docks knew that even when alongside they would be subject to relentless bomb attacks. Even if their own vessel was unscathed, the pressure on them as they watched ship after ship in their particular convoy burst into flames and sink to the bottom, often with no ship despatched to pick up survivors, was enormous. They fought on. If there was in fact a forgotten army it consisted of those who served at sea in the merchant service – forgotten often when survivors found themselves unpaid or widows received little support. Without their effort the nation would have collapsed. They too needed their sacrifice to be recognised.

I met David Parsons, the Director of the Merchant Navy Welfare Board, at one of the gatherings to commemorate the fiftieth anniversary of VE Day. David was immediately interested in the idea of the Arboretum and we soon came to an agreement not only that the project must pay tribute to the Merchant Navy but should do so in such a way that the enormity of its efforts throughout the Second World War be recognised. The logical way to do this was to plant a tree for every British-flagged merchant ship lost through enemy action in the war, but this would require many acres of land which we did not have. Luckily an ever willing Ron Foster at Redland Aggregate agreed to hand over another block of land, as yet unreclaimed, that would suit our purpose. A new boundary was drawn up to include a large hole which Paul Harrington was beginning to infill.

David Parsons's view that each lost ship should have its own tree proved a brilliant idea when it came to the matter of raising money for the merchant navy 'Convoy' as it soon became called. Armed with the Lloyd's list we were able to approach the shipping companies to ask if they would provide funding to commemorate each of their own losses. This was done through the Chamber of Shipping whose Director General, Admiral Sir Nicholas Hunt, I knew and whose offices were close to my own. The response was both immediate and sufficient. This great oak wood proved to be one of the easiest funding tasks we had to undertake.

As word spread among the merchant navy fraternity so individual groups indicated that they would like to take a more prominent role. Very soon the original concept of planting the right number of trees but not linking any tree to a particular ship had to be rejected, as shipping lines asked for their own Avenues, and Associations expressed interest in holding commemoration services at the site.

Among the first of these Associations was that linked to HMT *Lancastria*, a ship whose fate no less a person that Winston Churchill had tried to hide from the nation. Like many others, I had thought that once the last soldier was ferried away from the beaches of Dunkirk the evacuation of the British Army from France came to an end. This was not so. Stragglers continued to trek West hoping to reach ports in Normandy and Brittany from which they could be picked up. The last hope was St. Nazaire where thousands of servicemen and refugees gathered and prayed for a second miracle, which the arrival off shore of the troopship *Lancastria* must have indicated would happen. The ship spent several days loading thousands of evacuees, service and civilian, men, women and children. No one knows how many climbed on board, it may have been as many as 8,000, but their embarkation was noticed and reported to the German and Italian air forces.

When the bombs struck on 17 June 1940 there were far too many on board for an orderly abandonment so most found themselves in the water. Men like Lance Corporal Jim Leary who, after helping fire a Bren gun at the attacking planes, jumped off the ships for the first salt water swim of his life. It was not a pleasant experience for he, along with many others, was machine gunned by Italian fighter planes and also swallowed a copious amount of oil. He was rescued by the crew of a sailing dinghy and eventually transferred to the *Oronsay* for passage to the UK where he landed dressed fetchingly, and only, in a blanket, as his army issue underpants had swum down his legs and away as he lay on his back in the water.

The official casualty list states that 2,823 people died in the *Lancastria* disaster but most survivors and many historians believe that the number was nearer 4,000, with some surmising an enormous figure of 7,000. The exact number will never be known but, even the official figure represents the greatest loss of life in any allied shipping incident during the war. When news of the disaster reached Britain, whose inhabitants were still euphoric from the miracle of Dunkirk, Churchill ordered a press embargo so as not to dispel the national mood. From then on the survivors and the relatives of those who had been lost struggled to have their pain recognised by both the government and the nation. The planting of their own tree at The Arboretum was a small step in this process, and now every year a group gather in the clearing in which stands the HMT *Lancastria* tree and pay tribute to those who died in that great tragedy. A model of the ship was presented to the Arboretum by the Merchant Navy Welfare Board to help visitors understand the disaster that was the loss of *Lancastria*. Of course, every survivor had a tale to tell, mostly horrific. Staff Quarter Master Sergeant Fairfax recounted that, as the burning oil on the sea's surface surrounded two pals one of them drew a revolver from around his neck, shot his friend and then himself. Some witnessed happier endings; one wrote:

> Over yonder a woman, one of the few English civilians who were coming away in *Lancastria*, is calling out, 'My baby, look after my baby.' And back came the answer, 'It's all right, ma'am, we've got her.' And they have too, holding the baby well above the water.

Many years later a visitor to the NMA told one of the Friends that he had been responsible for rescuing that child but had heard no more about her until one day, quite unexpectedly, an invitation to her wedding arrived in the post. More frequently than might be anticipated the lump that rises in one's throat at the Arboretum is one of joy. There is, as might be expected of the British, also humour. Sapper Norman Driver, whose hobby was swimming, arrived home a survivor from the *Lancastria*, to be greeted by his father: 'How was it, son?' 'Pretty bad, the ship sunk and I ended up in the water.' 'That would have suited you.'

Another small group who wished to ensure that their shipping line and its losses were properly recorded were the Athel Line Apprentices (AAA). The Athel Line ran a small number of vessels from the West Indies to Britain, mainly importing fruit. Small though it might have been, it trained its own Deck Officers and had an *esprit de corps* which kept these men truly bonded for all the years of their retirement. One of them, Tom Gorst, a jolly, can-do sort of man, was determined that 'The Convoy' should be headed by ships from the Athel Line and set about to organise this. His plans included moving a large memorial boulder to the site along with several bollards from Liverpool docks which we hoped to re-erect on a low 'dock wall' in front of the trees. In the end the dock wall initiative failed for lack of funds, but the large bollards give the visitors a whiff of the sea as they approach the site.

Close to the Athel Line plot two of the trees linked to specific ships illustrate that the war at sea involved civilians and women and children as well as merchant seamen from many nations who were sailing under the British Flag. The plaque by the tree planted for the *Athenia* records the name of Miss Hannah Baird, a Canadian stewardess, as well as all her fellow voyagers who were lost. Although passenger liners fell prey to U-boat attack it was felt at the time that many children would be safer if they were evacuated to Canada and South Africa rather than remain in British cities which could be subjected to bombing raids. On 13 September 1940 the *City of Benares* sailed out of Liverpool for Canada with over eighty young evacuees on board. Four days out, with her escorts departed, silhouetted against a moonlit sky she became an easy prey to a single torpedo from *U-48*. When she came to plant the ship's tree at The Arboretum, Bess Cumming told us about the sixteen hours she had spent clinging to an upturned lifeboat in a cold Force 5 sea. Rescued, and recovering in one of the officer's bunks in HMS *Anthony*, but mourning her younger brother, she was amazed to find him clambering through the cabin door having being plucked from the sea some hours earlier. Not all siblings were blessed with such reunions. Seventy-seven children died including John Baker's elder brother, Bobby, who took off his own life-jacket and gave it to John, who has been haunted by that memory ever since. There were many civilian heroines as well, such as Miss Mary Cornish, one of the children's escorts, who kept her charges alive in their lifeboat by sheer force of character and determination, and the other carers in other evacuee ships whose now elderly charges remember them with great affection.

Once the scheme for the Merchant Navy 'Convoy' was publicised, the Honourable Company of Master Mariners decided that they too needed to be involved. One of their number, Chris Daniels, designed sun dials and he now proposed creating a large one in front of 'The Convoy' which would incorporated a chart of the world in stone, on to which would be imposed dots to show the position in which all these many ships had been lost. When, however, we came to draw a scale model of Chris's proposal it indicated that the Atlantic would just be a large blotch of coalesced dots so enormous were the shipping losses in those sea lanes. The chart was thus left just as an outline of the coasts.

When we drew up the Avenues and major plots for the Arboretum we had deliberately used a North East/South West orientation. This proved to be a brilliant layout for Chris's purpose because he was able to lay out his sun dial at the front corner of 'The Convoy' square pointing due South. In front of the sundial the Merchant Navy Welfare Board raised a plinth and a flag pole, adding a great dignity to the approach.

Chris's sun dial has no fixed gnomon; instead visitors are able to tell the time by their own shadow. Along the Greenwich Meridian were inscribed the months of the year. Standing at the appropriate month, visitors can read off the time from their shadow lying across an hour scale at the top. So accurate is the layout that it is possible to tell school children that the time that they were reading was a few minutes different from that on their watches because Lichfield lies some 76 miles further West than Greenwich. Having imparted this piece of information we then invited their teachers to explain the reason.

Almost every plot within the Arboretum engendered a spin-off or interest from a group of whom we knew nothing. The first of these linked to 'The Convoy' was a group who had served in Hospital Ships and Carriers, of which eight had been sunk during the war. The plaque for the Hospital Ships was a large one, probably as large as it could be and still remain free-standing, but some other Merchant Navy organisations were asking for us to list their ships and the dates and positions of their losses. This required far larger plaques that would need to be mounted on a base of some description. One afternoon, returning to Lichfield I saw a brick plinth beside the road. Parking on the nearby roundabout and hoping that the police were otherwise engaged, I jumped out, counted the bricks and quickly sketched the form. It proved to be ideal for all our requirements and, as a template, easy to cost and order, with the certain knowledge that a standard sized Blinford plaque could be made to fit them all.

These memorials, recording ships' names and other details, proved most popular and they were followed in turn by plinths raised to commemorate a number of Merchant Navy Training Ships. As these were being built we received a call from the Irish Republic drawing our attention to the fact that, although neutral, some thirteen Irish merchant ships had been sunk in the war, and asking us whether would we be willing to pay tribute to those ships and the 149 men who went down with them. Of course we were and felt very honoured so to do.

The date agreed for the dedication of 'The Convoy' involved us in a great gamble that almost did not pay off. It meant that no sooner had Harringtons finished restoring the site and levelling it than we needed to plant the trees in a vast area of bare earth. Luckily, suspicious as ever of the Midlands' weather, we erected a vast marquee in which to hold the Service, but this had to be approached along the unsurfaced Millennium Avenue, after which a hundred metres of bare ground lay between the tent and 'The Convoy' itself. The night before it bucketed. In the morning Millennium Avenue was a very long shallow swimming pool. The team scurried and cajoled and managed to bring in sufficient duckboards to lay a path to the marquee, which meant that the guests resembled the Children of Israel walking dry-shod between the waters of the Red Sea. A second set of duckboards, this time resembling those to be seen in pictures of the quagmires in the First World War trenches, was laid to the Merchant Navy flag pole. Everyone took the arrangement in good heart and the only casualty was the Chairman of the Merchant Navy Welfare Board who, having decided to drive down Millennium Avenue, went axle-deep in the mud as he tried to turn and leave.

With 'The Convoy' and the 'Naval Review' adjacent, it was felt that there needed to be a way of demonstrating the close link between these two groups of seafarers. For this reason the main avenue leading through the 'Review' and up to 'The Convoy' was named 'Pedestal Avenue' after the historic convoy which, after suffering great losses, brought vital supplies through to Malta during the war.

At the far end of 'Pedestal Avenue' in a small square was placed a naval Bofors gun gifted by another group whose activities linked both merchant and royal navies – the DEMS (Defensively Equipped Merchant Ships) gunners, naval personnel who, with the Maritime Royal Artillery, manned anti-aircraft weapons placed on important merchant vessels.

* * *

The first tree linked to the army, although planted for one of its smallest and most transitory of units, provided us with another lasting contribution. The Highland Fieldcraft Training Centre Association was established from 1943 to 1944 in Glenfeshie, Inverness-shire, with a winter camp at Poolewe. Its task was to take in soldiers who showed leadership potential and through robust outdoor training exercises realise this latent ability to enable them to be selected for officer training. As is so often the case with small organisations given a very positive role, the *esprit de corps* developed by the training staff was both high and enduring. This spirit was encapsulated in the Glenfeshie Prayer which was read at their dedicatory planting at the Arboretum on 17 May 1997 and was then used at the NMA on many similar occasions:

O Lord God, who didst send Thy Son into our world to share the labours and the hopes of men and to lead us forth to liberty and an ampler day, we set out from this place hallowed by the happy companionship of comrades in arms and a common cause, we would seek now to consecrate ourselves anew to the task that is set before us – even the salvation of our own and succeeding generations from oppression, cruelty, and the dominion of force.

For...all that we have...acquired to enable us to give richer and abler service...to remind us that Thou art the Creator of all that is clean and lovely and enduring; for the opportunity to serve Thee in the upholding of honesty and chivalry and fair dealing in the earth; for the fitness of body and mind, thy gift to us, and our desire humbly to lay our all upon Thine altar and the altar of our people's weal; for the bravery and the patience and the faith of those who walk the rough uneven way of life with us; for our own lives bought at the cost of life; and for the high mood of devotion to a cause bigger and better than self revealed in simple men and women around us – for all these we thank Thee as we now dedicate our life and talents to Thee.

Unto Thy keeping we dedicate ourselves, our country, our cause and our fairest hopes. We ask not that Thou wouldst spare us from danger, hardship or labour, but that we know the secret of life in glad and gallant and sacrificial service. When the day of our trial comes and the burden seems too heavy for us to bear, be Thou our comfort and strength and give us courage to endure to the end. For the sake of Jesus Christ Thy Son, our Saviour. Amen.

Written at the height of war for use by young men about to march towards the sound of the guns, the Glenfeshie prayer still has a message for many who gather in the calm of the Arboretum and who will depart to face the challenges of everyday life. Its continual use also illustrates another unique aspect of the project in that it was not the size or significance of any group that dictated the scale of their presence on the site but the effort that they made to ensure that they and their colleagues would be remembered. In this respect the staff and trainees of the Highland Fieldcraft Training Centre rank proudly alongside the Regiments, Divisions and Armies in which they fought.

The problem with designing an area for these major units of the Army was based primarily on gaining an understanding of the nature of the constituent parts of an organisation whose cap badges were only the present proud representation of a long, illustrious and complicated history. General Ramsbotham's letter requesting support was the key here, for we felt we had only to mark off each contribution as it came in to know if we were on the right track; but then we started to get donations from regiments whose names had not featured in the General's list and which we believed were no longer extant. Our great mentor at this stage was Ian Hallows's *Regiments and Corps of the British Army*, which gave us the story of amalgamations and name changes.

Our wish was to place the Regiments of Foot in a Parade of squares of trees, with each square, representing Regiments with close ties to each other. Thus the Royal Anglian Square had trees planted for the Royal Norfolk and Suffolk Regiments, the Royal Lincolnshire Regiment, the

Northamptonshire Regiment, The Bedfordshire and the Hertfordshire Regiment, the Essex and the Royal Leicestershires. The Light Infantry also had their square, as did the Queen's Regiment. In some cases, such as the Welsh Regiments, a square was not appropriate and their trees were placed in line. For the various Corps an Avenue of trees was planted running down one side of the Army Parade, and here units such as REME, the Army Air Corps and the Dental Corps were commemorated, as were the individual Corps that now made up General Ramsbotham's own unit, the Adjutant General's Corps, although very soon after we had begun planning, their Regimental Secretary contacted me with a view to creating their own Corps plot in addition to the single trees.

Although the Arboretum covered a large area, when it came down to planting individual plots space was at a premium. If we had left the choice to donors we would have planted ninety per cent oaks and little else. A mature oak can spread over a quarter of an acre of land shading all beneath it; if we were to provide a tribute to many and an interest to all we had to limit the number of oaks and nowhere more so than in the Regimental Squares. Indeed, if these were to look like a well formed body of men the last thing their trees needed to be was vase-like or spreading; what we needed were columnar, fastigiate trees. Luckily there were many fine examples from which to choose.

In some cases, such as the Cheshire Regiment, which actually had an acorn and oak leaves on its cap badge, we had no other choice; for others it was a case of studying their history and traditions. The officers of the Royal Tank Regiment had swagger sticks made of ash; the regimental magazine of the Royal Irish was called *Blackthorn*. In the case of the Welsh Regiments the great green bulk of Leyland Cypress, x *Cupressocyparis leylandi*, hated when in hedges, was an obvious choice, simply because it originated at Leighton Hall near Welshpool where it was spotted in 1926 by an American botanist on an evening stroll. It is thus one of the few great trees whose origins can be clearly stated as being in Wales. And it is a fine tree. So much has been written despairingly about it as a hedging plant that it might be worth quoting at length from that fine treesman, Alan Mitchell, who wrote in his *Trees of Britain*:

> For the big features, shelter and screens, Leyland Cypress forms have become the essential plants. Their ability to outgrow almost any plant on almost any soil in almost any situation makes them invaluable in the making of a new garden, defining the area, giving vital shelter and occasional single specimens or groups with extraordinary rapidity. Moreover, they are the favourite roost and nesting site for many garden birds...In short the arrival of the Leyland Cypress is a horticultural event on a par with the invention of the spade.

The Adjutant General's Corps, based at Winchester, had been formed from the amalgamation of the clerical, teaching, legal and discipline branches of the Army, to which had been added the Women's Royal Army Corps (WRAC). Unlike many of the older units their desire to have a plot was based on their need to establish their new identity. The idea, therefore, was to create a plot in which the amalgamated Corps were shown individually but planted together in unity. We had both the space and a design that would fit logically into it.

Between the Army Parade and the RAF Wings a broad path led down from Millennium Avenue to what was to be the United Nations plot. We planted this across the top with a screen of beech trees, similar to those that lined the approach to the Adjutant General's Corps Headquarters in Hampshire. They would later be pleached to resemble the West front of Winchester Cathedral, while a further ten trees, two for each of the original Corps, would form a rood screen between the AGC and the Staffordshire Regiment plot beyond.

The trees for the screen were fun to choose. Thus *Malus* 'Red Sentinel' was selected for the Royal Military Police; *Cupressus Sempervirens* 'Green Pencil' for the Clerks of the Royal Army Ordnance Corps; the flowering cherry, *Prunus* 'Spire', for the Educational Corps; *Malus* 'Wintergold' for the Pay Corps; a decorative pear, *Pyrus alixfolia* 'Pendula' (a 'downcast' pear showing miscreant repentance) for the Army Legal Corps; the green hazel, *Corylus Columna*, for the WRAC, whose regimental march was 'The Nut Brown Maiden' and whose leaf colour matched their uniform; finally, the Military Provost Staff Corps, were to have the ornamental apple *Malus* 'John Downie'.

Beyond the screen, the tribute to the local Staffordshire Regiment, whose Headquarters were only a few miles away at Whittington Barracks, was centred on four plane trees planted in a square whose measurements coincided with those of the four large transept pillars in Lichfield Cathedral. Among the tree planted within the plot for various units of the Regiment was one for Lance Corporal Coltman, the most highly decorated soldier in the British Army who was awarded the VC, DCM and bar and the MM and bar. His Victoria Cross was won towards the end of the First World War at Mannequin Hill in north-east France where, on 3/4 October 1918, as a stretcher bearer he went forward in fierce enfilading fire to recover a casualty who had been left behind during a retreat. Having dressed his wounds and brought him back, Coltman then repeated the dangerous mission of mercy three more times. So often Britain's highest award for gallantry has been awarded for those who, regardless of their own safety, have endeavoured to save others.

Several other Regiments and Corps felt that their members should be recalled not by just a single lone tree. Among these were, the Royal Army

Medical Corps (RAMC), the Royal Tank Regiment (RTR), the Royal Logistic Corps (RLC) and the Queen Alexander's Royal Army Nursing Corps (QARANC), the Royal Artillery (RA) and, most unexpectedly given our location, the Royal Irish Regiment. The RAMC decided to invite relations to have commemorative trees planted and it was soon obvious that the response was going to be too great to confine to one of our standard plots. We chose, therefore, to make an area of our matrix planting available to the Corps, in which we would further plant a collection of Acers. This would give us some wonderful autumn colours to attract the visitors and also the variety which we needed to introduce if the site was ever going to justify its claim to be an Arboretum and not a themed wood. Running down between these trees we planted an avenue lined with purple-leaved beech, each one dedicated to one of the corps' holders of the Victoria Cross. They would grow to form a wonderful end to the lengthy avenue that led from the visitor centre to frame the Chetwynd Bridge over the River Tame.

On the way to the RAMC Grove along 'The Beat' we created four open spaces. The first of these became the 'Mediterranean' bed but the remaining three were sponsored by Army Units: the Royal Logistic Corps (RLC), the Royal Tank Regiment and the Royal Irish. The first two were awkward plots to establish for not only did they lie at the lowest point of our badly draining Arboretum but behind them lay a stream that, when it rained heavily, took a short cut across the site to re-enter the River Tame directly across from these two plots. Although we built a drainage ditch it had to wait for the water levels in the Tame to drop before it could do its work and even then a shallow pond would be left across the RLC and Royal Tank plots. Given these conditions and the heavy downpours that were experienced during the planting phase, these two plots took the longest to become established at the site, and the patience of the Regimental Secretaries who had been the instigating enthusiasts in both their organisations was much appreciated.

The obvious trees to plant for the Royal Logistic Corps, which included the amalgamated units from the Army Catering Corps, Royal Corps of Transport, Royal Ordnance Corps, Royal Army Ordnance Corps and Courier Service, were those linked to food and provisions. The surrounding hedge was thus planted with fruit-bearing bushes such as blackberry, crab apple, hawthorn and rose, while fruit trees dominated the open area.

When we were told that the Royal Tank Regiment used to make its swagger sticks out of wood from ash trees we found an opportunity to plant a variety of ash within their regimental plot. We were even able to plant one tree brought over from Cambrai, the site of the first major tank offensive in World War One.

Most regiments wished their plot to be dedicated to all who had served under their colour without particular reference to any named individual. The Blues and Royals, however, felt that their plot should acknowledge the lives of all those who had served with them and lost their lives on active duty since 1945, which we were originally informed was some thirty-five individuals. Given this number it seemed logical to agree to planting a tree for each one of them. No sooner was this agreed than the number of losses was discovered to be ninety-three. Luckily the word 'blue' came to our rescue for there were a number of narrow, small trees with bluish foliage which would look stunning planted in line. The original plan had these planted in the shape of a large letter 'A' with at the apex a memorial stone and three Dawn Redwoods, *Metasequoia glyptostrodoides*, whose lance-like trunk was a most appropriate symbol for a cavalry regiment, each tree representing one of the three units that made up the present Regiment, the Royal Horse Guard, the Royal Dragoons and the Blues and Royals. Another senior grouping, the Household Division, asked that their plot be planted in the shape of their badge so that it could be seen from the air by officers flying themselves home for the weekend! We did so but never caught sight of a low-flying aircraft passing overhead.

The Royal Irish Regiment had been formed in 1992 by the amalgamation of the Royal Irish Rangers and the Ulster Defence Regiment, within which units lay concealed many other Regiments whose names are redolent of the history of the British Army. No foreign field has been left unstained by the blood of soldiers whose native land was the island of Ireland. Fierce and fearless, the Irish have won honour for their counties often in battles where against all odds they have triumphed or died valiantly in the attempt, such as on 'V' Beach at Gallipoli or on the first day of the Somme. The Project Officer for the Irish Infantry Grove, so called since the Regiment wished to ensure no unit was excluded by accident of nomenclature, Colonel James Linford, and his assistant WO2 Wyn Linton, were very wedded to the idea that the Irish contribution to the wellbeing of Britain should be acknowledged and that 'an acre of Ireland in the middle of the British Isles should be planted to commemorate the sacrifices of the Irish Infantry Soldier throughout history.'. The NMA was the obvious location for this. Yet we felt that the site should have Irish roots and so we selected for planting trees which were native to Ireland.

The plot was, therefore, hedged with Blackthorn, *Prunus spinosa*, which as well as providing wonderful white blossom in Spring was appropriate as its hard wood was used to make the swagger sticks of the Regiment's officers and senior NCOs. Within the enclosed square a path lined by Irish Yew, *Taxus baccata 'Fastigiata'*, was created, with further yew being used to form a shamrock shape.

When the last ice age covered the British Isles a small part of southern Ireland remained free of ice, and here oak tree survived the cold. A descendant of one of those oaks was now lifted and flown over to RAF Stafford for us to plant within the Irish Infantry Grove. It turned out to be larger than we expected and most of it stuck out over the back of our Land Rover as we drove slowly back to the Arboretum, where we spent many hours digging a hole large enough for it to be replanted. No other tree was watched as anxiously during its first few years as that oak which, although rather too large for transplanting, did settle down well in its new home.

The dedication of the Grove on 6 May 2000 was a most memorable occasion, but not before we were treated to a very Irish moment. Exactly one year earlier a minibus carrying a group of Regimental widows turned up at the NMA to attend the Service. When we told them, 'Right date, wrong year', they replied, 'Never mind, we were enjoying ourselves anyway. We'll come back next year!' And come back they did.

They came back to witness a great parade of soldiers marching to stirring regimental marches and then gathering to hear a most moving address from that great pillar of the Church, the Primate of All Ireland, the Very Reverend Lord Archbishop Eames. Just having this great churchman visit the Arboretum was a joy, to hear him speak in his melodious voice was ineffable and to have hundreds of Irish voices join together in singing 'Be thou my vision' took the congregation's voices higher than lark had ever flown above the NMA.

The complicated nature of the British Army, and our own lack of historical expertise, meant that we were often approached by organisations of whose existence we were unaware or had fragmentary knowledge, such as the old Yeomanry Regiments who had a proud history of service. Luckily we had planned a long Avenue to which no group had been assigned and this, planted with limes, became the 'Yeomanry Avenue'. On the bank beyond two units of the Indian Army, 'The Dogra' and 'The Baluch' had trees planted, the first organised by one of our earliest supporters, Colonel Ian MacDonald. Later this was added to by a plinth for the Sultan of Oman's Forces and a plot in the wavy shape of a Malayan kris for those who had served in that peninsula, making it very much an Asian area.

Most plots at the Arboretum were designed and developed in partnership, with the Arboretum coming up with the initial suggestion. In some cases, and the Royal Artillery was one, the design skills were wholly with the organisation itself. The Royal Artillery plot was the most ambitious undertaken to date at the site. It was designed around a waterfall and a pond by an artist member, Ray Hutchins, and reflected Ray's feeling for the landscape and its native trees. Ray also commissioned a pair of seats inspired by the gun carriage that forms the cap badge of the Royal Artillery.

These were cast at a nearby foundry but, sadly, on their way to the site on the back of an open lorry were decapitated as they passed under a low bridge. Rapid remedial work ensured that they were restored in time for the dedication service which was attended by well over a thousand serving and retired members of the Royal Artillery. Behind the plot, acting as a screen to the car parks, trees were planted in tribute to individual 'Gunners'.

* * *

The design of a 'Naval Review' had been straightforward. The concept of planting the Regiments of Foot in squares had been understandable, as had been the decision to form the Cavalry into a horseshoe. However, laying out the Royal Air Force plot presented us with a problem. It had started as a straightforward right-angled triangle with a curved hypotenuse, but the existence of a large bronze-age burial mound, conserved as an ancient monument, led to a large bite-size chunk being taken out at the base, leaving a very strange shape. Puzzling at the spot one day I happened to glance up a see a buzzard soaring overhead. For one moment its wing spread resembled the shape beneath it. A quick sketch and the RAF Wings were created. Once again, it was felt that the squadrons should be represented by a single species of tree, but the choice was not as singular as it had been for the Naval Review. However, silver birch seemed to be appropriate. On windy days, of which the Arboretum had many, the light branches would lift off as if wanting to fly while the tree trunk colour had a cloud-like quality. In due course we wanted to underplant with bluebell or ceanothus to give a sky effect as well; certainly the white of the trunks and the blue of ceanothus would look wonderful together.

The main groups to become involved with the Royal Air Force plot were Squadron Associations. We had originally intended that one wing of the planting should represent Bomber Squadrons and one Fighter but the designation of numbers appeared to be at best arcane and so it was decided to dedicate trees in as best a numerical order as it was possible to do bearing in mind there was no record of which squadrons had active associations or whether or not all those that did would want to have trees planted. However, all those that wished to have a commemorative tree wanted to hold a tree planting event at the site and soon we were holding regular RAF days with a short service in the Chapel followed by a few words at the site of the tree.

As with the prayer for the Royal Navy, these RAF Associations had their favourite reading, not a prayer, but the poem 'High Flight' by the Royal Canadian Air Force Pilot Officer John Gillespie Magee:

Oh! I have slipped the surly bonds of earth
And danced the skies on laughter-silvered wings;
Sunward I've climbed, and joined the tumbling mirth
Of sun-split clouds – and done a hundred things
You have not dreamed of – wheeled and soared and swung
High in the sunlit silence. Hov'ring there
I've chased the shouting wind along, and flung
My eager craft through footless halls of air.
Up, up the long delirious, burning blue,
I've topped the windswept heights with easy grace
Where never lark, or even eagle flew –
And, while with silent lifting mind I've trod
The high untresspassed sanctity of space,
Put out my hand and touched the face of God.

This must stand alongside Yeats' 'An Irish Airman Foresees his Death' as one of the two most evocative sonnets ever written about the war in the air.

A bible reading was not so easy, with few aircraft having been observed flying over the Holy Land in biblical times. Even though the Jews had a healthy distrust of all things nautical, the navy could at least turn to Psalm 107 to commemorate those that went down to the sea in ships.

However, a search uncovered some lines from Ecclesiasticus Chapter 51 which seemed to sum up the feeling of one trapped in a burning fuselage over enemy territory:

In the face of my assailants you came to my help;
in the fulness of your mercy and honour you rescued me from
  gnashing teeth waiting to devour me,
from hands that threatened my life, from the many troubles I
  endured.
From the choking fire enveloping me, from the flames I had not
  kindled,
From the deep recess of the grave, from the foul tongue and the lying
  word.
On every side I was surrounded and there was no one to help; I
looked for human aid and there was none.
Then I remembered your mercy, Lord, that you did in days long past;
  you deliver those who put their trust in you and free them from the
  power of their enemies.

Making each one of these dedications special for the group involved was an interesting exercise for our small band which included no one who had served in the RAF. Our preparations were helped greatly by the library staff at RAF Hendon who not only provided copies of the Squadron badges for us but also potted histories as well. It gave us knowledge and involvement enough to avoid any solecisms but also a feeling that we had, for one brief moment, joined with those who had gathered to remember their colleagues who could no longer be with them. And, of course, the research gave us yet another insight into the level of sacrifice that had been made by pilots and aircrew during the second world war.

And the losses continued. Shortly after the Iraq war ended Jackie was contacted by a family wishing to have a tree planted to commemorate their son, a pilot shot down by friendly fire during the conflict when returning from a mission. The recent nature of their loss made the event one of the saddest in the Arboretum's short history but it also demonstrated that the project had a present and ongoing purpose.

Of course, a wing for Bomber and a wing for Fighter Command, excluded many other groups involved in the history of the Royal Air Force. Many air stations had also made contributions and it was planned for their trees to surround the main wings, providing shelter and a framework.

Coastal Command's involvement began with another group of which few of a new generation had knowledge – the Indian Ocean Flying Boat Association which was formed as late as 1988 to bring together those who had served during the Second World War in fifteen RAF Squadrons together with 413 Squadron Royal Canadian Airborne and 321 Royal Netherlands Air Force. Flying mainly in those elegant dowager duchesses of aircraft, the Catalina and Sunderland flying boats, from over thirty stations and bases between Aden and Penang, theirs was another story of derring-do and the triumph of mechanical ingenuity over the deadening hand of distances. Day after day they scanned the vast blue desert for enemy U-Boats which they then engaged, with the latter sometimes on the surface firing much larger calibre weapons back at them. The date of formation of the association was not unusual. Before becoming involved with the Veterans I had imagined that most of their groups would have been set up shortly after the war ended so that they could get together and discuss the deeds they had wrought. Not a bit of it. Two things became very apparent: firstly, the reticence and associated modesty of those who had done great things and witnessed historic, and often unpleasant action at first hand; secondly, that these associations were not created to give an outlet for old yarns but mainly to provide a support organization for comrades as age began to wear them down. We, of the lucky generation who have not had to come together to challenge the world for our survival, have few such groupings and may well find our seventh age less pleasing to pass through.

There seemed to be only one spot suitable for planting trees in tribute to those who landed and took off from water and that was overlooking a long stretch of the River Tame and the lake beyond. Once the Flying Boats were here it was not long before Coastal Command itself landed alongside in the adjacent plot.

Between the Flying Boats and the RAF Wings, on a bank overlooking the latter, was planted a tribute to another group whose contribution to our future could be forgotten because they were a hostilities-only outfit. This was the RAF Servicing Commando who were the first of the Special Forces Groups that were to become very involved at the Arboretum. Servicing Commando units were set up between 1942 and 1943 from groups of 'tough technicians' who were required to move into a contested area as soon as sufficient land existed to set up a temporary airstrip, often having to dig themselves in first to repulse a counter attack; a task which, according to their website, the 'old soldiers performed automatically and the young ones as soon as the shells began to fall near them.' In Normandy a Unit was landed on 7 June and had the first airfield operational by 10 June. Other units carried out similar work in Italy, North Africa and the Far East. For the Servicing Commando we planted a collection of Acers as we felt these could represent all the areas in which they had served. However, like the silver birch they were difficult to get going and also suffered a high failure rate.

There seemed to be no reason why silver birches should prove difficult to establish as they are by nature colonizers and tolerant of wet conditions. Yet, Spring after Spring, we watched with growing gloom as tree after tree failed to burst into green leaf. We got very used to scratching away a strip of bark with our thumb nails only to see the brown sign of dead wood rather than the green of living sap. Nevertheless, sufficient remained alive for us not to despair and we replanted with better success. Once this area is well established, a gentle breeze moving through the branches on a sunny day will make the RAF 'Wings' one of the most beautiful plots within the Arboretum. Standing there in the bucolic pleasantness of central England one will have an idea of what so many wanted to live for and were prepared to die to retain. The tales of what they achieved will be remembered by fewer and fewer standing there, but the badges of the squadrons will encourage those that wish to do so to go away and research the achievements of the great names of Cheshire, Gibson, Bader and their colleagues. Like the chargers on which Henry V's knights were mounted the names of Spitfire, Hurricane, Lancaster and Beaufort will be recalled and their characteristics and fiery spirits brought back to life. And, as medieval coats of arms, the squadron badges will proclaim the greatness of 617 and 627 squadrons and names like Dam Busters and

Pathfinders and Biggin Hill will compete with Agincourt and Crecy to tell of the winning of great renown and the delivery of great deeds.

Away from the main Royal Air Force section two large plots were dedicated by the RAF Halton Apprentices and the RAF Regiment. The Halton Apprentices, whose alumni included a few Royal Naval personnel, were one of the earliest and keenest groups to be involved and the one which had the simplest solution to raising money for their plot; they asked each class that had passed through the apprentices' training college to make a donation. It worked well as did the design for their plot. Ahead of graduation each apprentice was required to demonstrate his skills by turning out a four-bladed propeller in brass based on their trade badge. Using *lonicera nitida* 'Baggesen's Gold', we recreated this form and surrounded it with a low hedge of the same species of honeysuckle in the evergreen version. In the surrounding space a number of trees were planted including one for Sergeant Thomas Gray who was awarded a posthumous Victoria Cross for pressing on with a bombing attack over the Albert Canal in May 1940 while under exceptionally heavy fire.

Over the way from the Halton Apprentices the RAF Regiment had their plot. From the start they wanted a stone plinth as the central feature, and this was duly commissioned. For the arboreal element of their plot I proposed that we represent the launch pad of Rapier missiles, with which the Regiment defended airfields, by planting four clusters of four columnar *Prunus* 'Amanogawa', with its beautiful and fragrant dense semi-double blossoms born on compact and erect stems – a choice tree. The other arboreal link that we were able to create for the RAF Regiment was through planting two Dawn Redwoods, *Metasequoia Taxodiaceae*, for these trees were not discovered until 1941 which was very close to the date at which the Regiment itself was established. Dawn Redwoods, which are deciduous conifers, have wonderful deeply grooved trunks which reach straight up and taper to a fine point at their summit. No arboretum should be without this exceptional tree so it was wonderful to have an excuse to plant it in our own.

Although most of the armed forces' plots were linked to an individual service several had a tri-service 'purple' basis. There were not too many of these but two in particular we were glad to welcome because of the work they did and whom they represented. So often in any conflict the public seem to echo Rudyard Kipling's words, 'It is only your dead that count', while paying scant attention to the injured who are so often a more numerous group. 'Injured' covers a vast range of personal damage and the severity is not often referred to nor the suffering involved highlighted. One group that made its objective the care for the injured was BLESMA, the British Limbless Ex-Servicemen's Association, who celebrated their seventy-fifth anniversary at the NMA. For BLESMA we had created a plot with two paths in the shape of a cross, along the sides of which we planted narrow fruit trees which could be pruned and plucked by someone in a wheel chair. It proved to be very popular, and for their anniversary another group of trees were added alongside Giffard Avenue, named after an early and active member of BLESMA who had also been a leading member of the Country Landowners' Association in Staffordshire.

That path between the Visitor Centre and the Chapel was lined with aromatic shrubs, planted in the shape of eyes, in tribute to another group of veterans who had suffered from the cruelties of war – the blinded, whose plight was the special concern of St. Dunstan's, a home that helps with those who have received that most challenging of war wounds. For what was very apparent to all those involved in creating the Arboretum was that Britain's history and global responsibilities meant that there were few theatres of conflict around the world in the twentieth century in which our service men and women would not have a part to play in the twenty-first.

CHAPTER FOUR

Cypress and Eucalyptus: Theatres of War

Know ye the land where the cypress and myrtle
Are emblems of deeds that are done in their clime?
Where the rage of the vulture, and the love of the turtle,
Now melt into sorrow, now madden to crime?

Lord Byron

Ray Pell was scared. He had not had time to be so in the previous frenetic hours. Shortly after digging in beside a stone bridge near the little Dutch town of Wuustwezel his unit, the First Battalion, the Leicestershire Regiment (part of 49 West Riding Infantry Division, 'the Polar Bears') had come under a surprising and intense German attack that brought apple trees crashing to the ground around Ray as he dashed through the orchard to drag a badly wounded young colleague into the comparative and temporary shelter of a conservatory where, although the glass shattered above them, the thin low brick wall gave some protection. When the firing intensified, the two men barged into the house and were bustled down into the basement by the owner to join his family, including their mortally wounded daughter. By now enemy tanks were passing by and soon it was obvious that the Germans were conducting a house-to-house search. Ray and his friend were hastily bundled under a mattress on top of which the lady of the house perched herself. Hoping that the dust, smoke and smell of cordite would neither make him sneeze or his friend cry out in pain, Ray lay still while a German soldier, armed with a machine gun came down the steps; but to his shouted question as to whether they were any English soldiers down there, the brave householder shouted back, 'No'. Satisfied, the German moved away.

By evening, the young soldier had died, and Ray and two companions who had been sheltering with him decided that they had to try and rejoin their Battalion. Very, very nervously they stumbled through a field of enormous cabbages until they reached a road that they presumed led towards their own lines. But how to be recognised as friends? Their answer was to sing with all the gusto they could manage, 'Roll out the Barrel', until an English voice invited them to shut up.

But having rejoined, Ray was to participate in even more terrible events than he had experienced so far. Sent out on the grim task of recovering the bodies of his slaughtered comrades, he had the heartbreaking experience of dragging a body out of a ditch to find that it was that of the friend who had been the best man at his wedding the previous February. A little while later they discovered their own anti-tank position which had been blown apart. In an effort to ensure these men had a decent burial, Ray's team toiled around the site trying to reassemble complete bodies from the scattered limbs, heads and torsos. That horrendous duty over they moved down the road and came across the bodies of another nine of their wounded companions which had been laid in a line and then run over by a German tank.

In a matter of days Ray had gone through the whole range of experiences that could befall the 'poor bloody infantry'. Even after the fighting had moved away from Wuustwezel, there was a savage final act. In January 1945, a German flying bomb, aimed at Antwerp, fell short of its target and ploughed into the house where Ray had hidden, killing the Visser family who had sheltered him.

I have no idea whether these experiences profoundly altered Ray's character or not but, when I met him in 1995, I was immediately struck by the gentleness of this big man who was determined to perpetuate the memory of his friends and all who had served with 49 Div.

Ray called at our office to discuss planting a tree, something which he had discovered had been done by 59 Division, the Friends of Thierry Harcourt, who had brought over a mature beech from the town that they had liberated. By this time I was concerned that we were planting too many trees and we needed to think about other forms of memorial which would take up less space and provide variety. It was a hot day and the pub over the road was invitingly close. We adjourned.

Over the first pint Ray told me the story of 49 Div and how they had received their badge and title, 'The Polar Bears', after service at the beginning of the war in Norway and Iceland, from where they returned to take part in the Normandy invasion. Might we, I suggested, have a sculpture of a polar bear instead of a tree? Ray liked the idea and, over the second pint sketched out possible designs. We soon had the idea of standing the bear on a three legged plinth which, after the third pint, we agreed would look better if it took the form of an iceberg. Ray, who once the idea was agreed never had any anxiety about its delivery, did have one concern – vandalism: would the memorial attract graffiti artists? With that worry at the back of his mind we went to see Peter Benson, Chairman of the British Wood Carvers' Association, and a near neighbour of Ray's in Essex. Peter's answer to the vandalism worry was to suggest that the Polar Bear be made so big, life-size, and raised so high that it would be vandal proof. What is more, he was prepared to form a team to build the bear out of yellow hard wood, an extremely durable timber that would weather but not rot. We now had to find someone to build a plinth and a base for it.

Among the many practical voluntary organisations in Lichfield who were willing to assist the Arboretum in whatever way they could, the local Rotarians were pre-eminent. One of their number, David Radcliffe, offered to act as the structural engineer and to advise on the design, and another put us in contact with the bricklaying Instructor, Bill Bragger, at nearby Burton Technical College. Another delight in the creation of the Arboretum was coming across people whom one asked to walk a mile only to discover they were prepared to keep going over every awkward hill and through every slough until the job was thoroughly finished. Having asked the College for assistance, they took on the building of the large circular brick plinth as a challenge for their students and a project with which they were delighted to be involved. What is more, and very importantly, they were prepared to do the work for free. Thus, through these many kindnesses, a memorial that was costed at £225,000 was built with the ever-optimistic Ray Pell assisted by his son-in-law, another Ray, managing to raise £14,000 of this in cash; the rest was covered by gifts in kind given, it must be said, because Ray was a man to whom people could not say no, so great an empathy could his spirit and his mission engender in others.

Down in Billericay, Peter Benson and his Essex woodcarving team, after much research, began work on the bear, which was to be of a laminate construction so that the timber could stretch and shrink in response to temperature changes and wet weather without distorting or cracking. They took on more besides. The design allowed for the badges of all the units that formed part of 49 Div to be displayed on the plinth. This was an intricate and potentially lengthy process. To get it done in time Peter asked wood-carving colleagues throughout the country to carve the badges – about 100 volunteered so to do.

On 20 May 1998, the well oiled nine foot long and five foot high, two and a half ton Bear was ready to be move to the Arboretum where another dedicatory service, the opening of the George Cross Island plot, in the shape of a Maltese Cross, was planned to end in time for the Bear's arrival. In these pre-mobile phone days it was easy to monitor its progress: the traffic bulletin on Radio 5 kept including information along the lines of:

'Motorists, heading North along the M 1 / M6 should take care, as there is a slow moving Polar Bear on the inside lane!'

As our Service finished, the Bear arrived, giving the congregation an additional event by which to remember their day. There was a moment of nervousness when the Bear was lowered to see whether the holes in its paws matched those drilled in the plinth to receive the spigots – they did.

On 7 June 1998 the Right Reverend John Bickersteth, the former bishop of Bath and Wells and an ex-member of 49 Div, conducted the dedicatory service to welcome formally the Polar Bear to what was still a muddy field. It was a strange day, baking sunshine and frequent thunderstorms, so that everyone from Bishop to Bear spent periods getting drenched and then steaming dry. Over a thousand people came to the Service and a very proud contingent of Veterans led by the present day Band and Colour Party of 49 Div staged a wonderful march past. But one of the great memories of the day was that of a young girl, Jodie Johnson, in school uniform reciting a poem that she had written at the age of nine. It was called, 'Fifty Years Late':

> I am only a child
> And it's hard to explain,
> The feelings I have,
> As I sit in the rain,
> And think of the men
> Who went off to war,
> Knowing that they would not
> Come home anymore.
>
> I cannot say thank you
> To the men left in France,
> Who laid down their lives
> To give me a chance,
> I cannot say thank you
> To the ones who returned,
> For thank you is not
> What those brave men earned.
> I owe them my life,
> As I live it today,
> A life lived in freedom
> Because of that day.
> I owe them much more
> Than I can ever repay,
> I owe them the lives

That they gave up that day.
They will live in my heart
For as long as I live,
And my children will learn
Of that gift that they give.

So impressed had Ray been with Jodie's poem that he had organised for it to be included, along with another poem, 'Who are these men?', written when she was eleven, among the regimental badges that were placed around the plinth. Copies of it proved a best seller at the Arboretum, the proceeds going to help with the maintenance of the Bear that had been so well built that, apart from minor dentistry and a pedicure, it endured the worst that the sodden Midlands could throw at it with all the stoicism that you would expect from such an animal and the men whose badge it was.

Sadly, the story of the Polar Bear would not be complete without recounting events that followed the unveiling. All through the complicated process of its creation Ray had kept meticulous notes and tape-recordings of meetings as well as briefing and getting approval from the 49 Div Association Committee for his work and decisions. Now, with the job done, a small coterie demanded changes, most of which would have required major alterations to the structure. It is hard to see why this criticism surfaced when it did except to say that jealousy may have played a part. Anyway, at the time of the next Polar Bear reunion, which Jackie Fisher was to address in Nottingham, she was met by the Brigade Commander when she arrived, who informed her that Ray had just had a heart attack and died shortly before the meeting convened, while he was defending himself against some harsh criticism. It was the saddest privilege of my life to conduct his funeral service some days later. On that day we said goodbye to a gentle, lovely man who had dedicated his life to the memory of his wartime colleagues and achieved a memorial that will be reverenced and enjoyed, an unusual combination, for many years to come.

The dedication of the Polar Bear was at that time by far the largest event that we had staged on the site. We would not have managed it successfully had it not been for the volunteer support of our new 'Friends of the National Memorial Arboretum' organisation, ably assembled by Carol Davis-Lee and directed by Jackie Fisher. From then on the Friends became an integral and vital part of our team whenever any major event was planned for the site.

For several years the Polar Bear gazed out across the Arboretum with not much to keep him company; the trees had to grow and the roads and buildings had yet to be constructed. Before the drainage was improved he often had to stand, in both winter and summer, on his small brick 'iceberg' surrounded by water (a forewarning of global warming?). Somehow he seemed at home in that setting, and if the Arboretum could have a favourite memorial the Polar Bear would probably be it. After the Polar Bear was unveiled the Essex Woodcarvers remained involved with the project to our great benefit. Not only would they produce a number of wonderful carvings but Peter Benson had decided that the Arboretum would make an ideal centrally placed location for members of his woodcarvers' association to hold their annual conference; so, for a fortnight every summer, the Visitor Centre was filled with the creative work of skilled carvers from around the country, always including a few polar bears.

Dunkirk

Ray's Polar Bears had been evacuated from Norway by sea and later, although not on D-Day itself, had returned to Europe via the Normandy beaches. Their experiences thus mirrored the two most famous amphibious operations of the Second World War – Dunkirk and Normandy.

At the Arboretum we decided that these two major events should be honoured in a most prominent place. The front of the Arboretum seemed the best site, for along here we could plant an Avenue redolent of the long ones in France down which British troops headed both West and East. One continuous Avenue of Poplars, kindly donated by the Poplar Tree Company, was thus planted, with the West end dedicated to the Dunkirk while the eastern extension paid tribute to those who had served in Normandy.

As we developed the idea so the modesty of the survivors, members of the two Associations, became most apparent. They could not believe, and took a lot of persuading so to do, that the Arboretum was being planted in tribute to all who served, not only those who had lost their lives but those who had come safe home as well. The latter, of course, included many injured both in body and mind and to whom few war memorials pay tribute. The leaves of the trees along the Dunkirk/Normandy Avenue shimmered for them all.

By the time the ground was ready for the official dedication of the Dunkirk Avenue many of the members of the Veterans' Association were well past their eightieth year. They decided, therefore, that their Service at the Arboretum would be the last official gathering of the Association as a whole, although individual branches could, of course, continue to meet. Thus, we were again humbled by a significance which we were proud to acknowledge.

The dedication of the Dunkirk trees was one of the site's earliest major events which involved catering on site as well as running a parade. Many individual initiatives were called upon to give the appearance of calm as hired generators packed up and sound systems uttered not a squeak. Very aware of the age of the many hundreds of Veterans who had assembled, we made sure we had sufficient Red Cross coverage, and their services were called upon: a sixteen year old Sea Cadet fainted – the Veterans needed no help and every one of them insisted on taking part in the march past. Long after the official events had drawn to a close and most of the Veterans had departed one of the few remaining came along to report that he had been leaning over a portaloo when his medals had fallen off, in and under a very full receptacle. It was left to Jackie Fisher literally to roll up her sleeves, once the day was over, to recover the by now gleaming medals from the loo, and post them on to the delighted veteran. The event almost speaks for itself but it does illustrate very well how willing and dedicated were the small group of volunteers who helped create the Arboretum. Frank Kent, himself an elderly Veteran, used to stand out in the car park, whether it was muddy or dusty, whether the weather was fine or rainy, directing traffic throughout an event; whoever was available used to clean up accidents in the lavatories; everyone took a turn at serving food and washing up. No one ever refused to do a job however menial. And, somehow, the messier the task the more mirth it engendered.

When the enormity of the task of lifting the members of the British Expeditionary Force from the beaches of Dunkirk ahead of the advancing victorious Germans became apparent the British Government called upon skippers of private vessels to sail across the Channel to help with the ferrying of troops from the beaches to the larger vessels lying off shore. The response was magnificent and the 'Little Ships', as they became known, claimed a justified place in the pantheon of heroic British actions. Some years after the war Raymond Baxter, a popular broadcaster and owner of one of these little ships, conceived the idea of forming an Association to which the ships that took part, rather than their owners, would belong. As the boats ranged from shrimpers to gin palaces the Association took on a most eclectic appearance both of boats and owners. On major anniversaries the ships would gather at Dover to repeat their glorious and successful passage to Dunkirk. When one saw how small some of the craft were one realises that the calm sea was a very important ingredient in the miracle of Dunkirk. The spirit of those boat owners also gripped the imagination of that wonderful story teller, Paul Gallico, and his short novel *The Snow Goose* tells the tale of a man who made the journey accompanied by a snow goose whom he had befriended.

We felt that the Dunkirk area should also pay homage to the Little Ships, and it was a wonderful discovery to find that there was a small spire-like cherry, *Prunus* 'Snow Goose', that was admirably suited for planting in front of the poplars, thus encouraging visitors not only to find out more about the Little Ships but to read Gallico's charming book.

Many years ago I saw a picture of the Dunkirk beaches that just showed a rifle plunged into the sand with a helmet hung over it. Perhaps it marked a grave, the caption did not say, but from then on that photograph became for me an icon of the event. When I mentioned this to the Dunkirk Veterans they thought it would be a good idea to recreate that symbol on site. We agreed on a division of labour whereby I would get some sand from Dunkirk while they got hold of the rifle and helmet. Luckily, by this time Redland Aggregates had been taken over by Lafarge, a French company, and the new firm's lorries were frequently crossing the Channel. They agreed to divert a truck to Dunkirk to scoop up, with the mayor's permission a load of sand from the beach. A simple but telling memorial was thus created of an event the horror of which cinema goers have recently been reminded by the film *Atonement*.

Normandy

For the Normandy Veterans we felt that the five landing beaches, Gold, Juno, Sword, Utah and Omaha should be mentioned as part of their plot. This time the logistics and funding involved in bringing sand over from each of these beaches in a meaningful quantity proved too much for us, although it is hoped that this can be done at some future date. Instead we organised five large boulders to be placed before the Avenue, on each of which would be engraved jut the single name of a beach.

The dedication of the Normandy Veterans' Avenue took place on a blustery day that followed on from a very wet week. As the Service progressed it became obvious that the attention of many of the Veterans was being distracted by something happening behind the drumhead party. Glancing around I saw that one of the lorries delivering infill to build the mound on which the visitor centre was to be built had slewed off the track and was suspended at a precarious angle over the bank. The driver and the mud had the good sense to remain in equilibrium for the duration of the Service or we would have lost many of the Veterans to that alternative entertainment. As it was, with the service complete many moved over to photograph the lorry before returning to record their own memorial.

Arnhem

Another Avenue at the Arboretum was planted for what for many of the post-war generation has become, thanks to the film, *A Bridge Too Far*, one of the most remembered events of the second world war: Operation Market Garden, the attempt to seize a Rhine crossing intact. The Veterans of that campaign were one of the first groups determined that their efforts should be brought to the attention of all who visited the NMA. The Market Garden Avenue was thus one of the first to be planted and its thirteen small-leaved limes, *Tilia cordata*, one for each Branch of the Association, grew far faster than the same species did along Millennium Avenue, doing much to keep us convinced that the project would succeed during the early dismal winters and damp summers. The plaque created to tell the story of

Operation Market Garden was also one of the first produced of its size and again showed that much information and emotion could be contained on a very small area of metal. It showed a map of the operational area and carried a brief account of the campaign to seize the river Rhine crossing at Arnhem and help shorten the war. What it did not have room for were the words written by Field Marshal Montgomery to General Urquhart on 28 September 1944 shortly after the operation ended:

> There can be few episodes more glorious than the epic of Arnhem, and those that follow after will find it hard to live up to the high standard that you have set. So long as we have in the armies of the British Empire officers and men who will do as you have done, then we can indeed look forward with complete confidence to the future. In years to come it will be a great thing for a man to be able to say, 'I fought at Arnhem.'

In creating Market Garden Way we had the privilege of meeting many of those men. They were proud, and justly so.

The Mediterranean

Most of us are taught to drive by nervous relations or phlegmatic driving instructors. Edwin Horlington had to teach himself – and in a hurry. With the German army advancing rapidly on Athens and about to encircle the allied forces that had gathered in the city, Edward was placed, in the middle of the night, beside a one ton truck and asked if he could drive. His truthful negative went unheeded. He was told to jump in, follow the truck in front, and adjust his speed by moving the right hand pedal up and down. He was also informed that the vital stores in the back must not on any account fall into German hands. The fact that his maiden driving lesson was also taking place during a black out in which no vehicle was allowed to use headlights added to the challenge, although adjusting to driving on the wrong side of the road was not a problem for someone who had never driven at all. After bumping into the vehicle ahead for the first few miles Edward discovered what the gear lever was for, but this advance was negated by his driving into a ditch by the side of a bridge. He made it eventually to Kalamata where an evacuation was underway, and it was here that he discovered that his precious cargo consisted of jars of rum, tinned fruit and packets of cigarettes. These were soon sniffed out by an undisciplined throng and the truck made lighter.

Although many of the troops were resigning themselves to surrender. Edwin was determined to escape. He recorded: 'Many men, including me, tried swimming out to distant boats ... some of them had rafts, driftwood and the like for support. Many drowned and the shouts and screams were unforgettable.' The scene at Kalamata was indeed hellish as ship after ship was bombed and set alight or sunk in the harbour approaches. The Royal Navy tried its utmost, but the lack of air cover led to heavy losses. A short while later similar naval losses, while trying to evacuate the Army from Crete, led to the suggestion that the fleet should abandon its colleagues ashore. The response took the form of one of the most memorable of naval messages when Admiral Cunningham, Commander-in-Chief, Mediterranean, signalled: 'It takes three years to build a ship, it takes three hundred to build a tradition. The evacuation goes on.'

Edwin eventually got picked up by HMS *Hero* and was disembarked in Egypt suffering from pneumonia, shock and exposure. He always considered himself to be one of the lucky ones and after the war founded the Brotherhood of Veterans of the Greek campaign, to perpetuate the memory of those who had died and to offer fellowship to those who survived and their relatives. For many years the Brotherhood made annual pilgrimages to Kalamata where they were welcomed as heroes by the Greeks. All of them, however, retained their modesty, but their memories were always tinged by the feeling that they had been let down, even abandoned, by their superiors and the politicians who had placed them in harm's way in the first place. Many thought that the description of those days was told far better through the fiction of Evelyn Waugh's *Sword of Honour* trilogy than any official account.

The Brotherhood was the first of many first group of Veterans who wished their deeds to be recalled at the NMA. Having witnessed what they had during the Greek campaign theirs was an association with no formal structure. This was not to say they were either disorganised or unenthusiastic. Each year they held a reunion in Leamington Spa, which meant that they were sufficiently close to the Arboretum to bus over for a dedicatory Service on site. But they wanted more than a single tree. We thought it would be appropriate and fit in with our developing design to create an open air Chapel based on the small Greek orthodox ones which the Veterans would have seen on so many hill tops and in every village as they retreated.

The design for their Chapel was based around a low hedged 'wall' in front of which four pillars of cypress, *Cupressus sempervirens*, so redolent of the Greek countryside, would stand, although it took some while for these to become established on a windswept, waterlogged site which would not have reminded their roots of home. Inside the Chapel was placed a large boulder with a plaque explaining the story of the Veterans, written in both English and Greek while, at the East end a small altar was erected. When the day of dedication came, two Greek orthodox priests from Birmingham, neither of whom spoke English, played a central, and lengthy, role as they chanted away in Greek and made sure that every part of the Chapel was sprinkled with holy water. By the time it came for our bugler to play Last Post and Reveille we had to pause while he unfroze his fingers.

The main plot recalling the Mediterranean campaigns lay across 'The Beat' from the Greek Chapel. This was a double square which recalled very much the shape of the Mediterranean Sea itself. With this in mind we planned to recreate the North African littoral and its stony desert using the raw material which Redland Aggregates were quarrying right alongside the site. To prepare the North Africa Plot we took large rolls of mypex and pegged them onto the ground to form the outline of the map from Oran to the Suez Canal. On to this the stone would be dumped once Redland could find time to deliver. In the meantime the mypex was held down with clods of earth. They were not adequate. Arriving at the Arboretum early one morning I found Sam Kent, himself a North African veteran, with one hand gripping Tobruk and the other hanging on to Benghazi, trying desperately to prevent North Africa getting airborne and landing on Italy in an unparalleled seismic upheaval of tectonic proportions. Sam, who was several years over eighty at the time, seemed determined to cling on even if it meant a precarious magic carpet trip. I leapt over the fence and together we calmed the bucking black sheeting and got the land to settle back in place. Yet again, one of our volunteers had saved the day. That afternoon Redland delivered and a stony desert took shape in the green Staffordshire countryside.

Into this desert we planted a number of trees to represent important geographical locations: Cairo, El Alamein, Oran and Tobruk. The latter was very important as the 'Desert Rats ' were very keen to have their colleagues and their exploits remembered at the Arboretum, so much so that when they stood down as an organisation they laid their standard to rest at the Chapel.

The Tobruk survivors illustrated another good reason why the Arboretum was so important and needed to be as inclusive as possible. The story of the siege of Tobruk, its fall and recapture is an epic tale and one that shows fighting men in a proud light. It is true that it had neither the horror nor longevity of Stalingrad or Leningrad, but in the annals of British military history it is well worthy of standing comparison with Lucknow and Ladysmith. Yet, in the overview of history that is the lot of most who belong to younger generations, the siege of Tobruk gets no mention. This is not to deprecate either the teaching of History or the interests of youth, it is merely to state a fact. There is no space in national curricula to dwell on such events, however gallant the participants were. How important it is, therefore, to tease the enquiring mind at such places as the Arboretum where several generations of the same family might be persuaded to discover more about their past by asking the question, 'Tobruk? What went on there then?'

There were two main groups associated with the Africa plot area. The first was the First Army Association, encouraged by the daughters of their founder, and the other was a small group of signallers who belonged to the 5 (London) Corps Signals Old Comrades Association. Under the guidance of their Chairman, Dennis Roberts CBE, they had become another association which punched above their weight. Dennis was to continue his involvement by organising the General Post Office plot for, like so many individuals interested in the Arboretum, his long life had revolved around several relevant organisations.

At the Tobruk spot on the North Africa plot we planted two *Cupressus sempervirens*, while elsewhere there was room for two types of African cedar, *Cedrus atlantica* and *Cedrus libani* and the holm oak, *Quercus ilex*. Here, in a slightly sheltered position, we hoped that they would manage to grow successfully, which they did.

To fit Italy as well as North Africa into the Mediterranean bed meant that we had to manoeuvre the Italian peninsula and Sicily through ninety degrees so that they lay parallel to the African coast. This gave us a very lengthy peninsula along which to plant trees. Here the badge of the Italy Star Association dictated the planting plan, for on it were named the major battles of that long campaign that began with the landings in Sicily in 1943. Thus we planted a tree each for Sicily, Taranto, Anzio, Salerno, Sangro, Foggia, Ancona, Coriano, Argenta, Florence, Bologna, the Po Valley and Cassino, names the mention of which brought memories of bitter fighting back to each of the Veterans. As well as *Cupressus Sempervirens*, we included two types of Mediterranean pine, *Pinus nigra* and *Pinus pinea* here, hoping that the shady garden that they created would bring a sense of peace as well as recall the exhortation of the Italy Star Association:

> When you walk in peaceful lanes so green,
> Remember us, and think what might have been.

Between Italy and North Africa we had space to plant a memorial to an island which never required liberating because its inhabitants and defenders fought so tenaciously to keep it free – Malta, whose gallantry was recognised by the whole island being awarded the George Cross. Of course, Malta was used to being besieged and among its earlier defenders had been those who wore another great cross, that of the Knights of Saint John. To make an appropriate memorial we therefore created an outline of that eight pointed cross whose very shape reflected the many peninsulas of the island; we also left the cross hollow so that the shelter of Grand Harbour could be reflected in the design. The dedication on 23 June 1999 by the Reverend John Williams, Chaplain to the Forces, was yet another occasion in those early years when special paths had to be laid to help the guests reach the site of the service without slipping above their ankles in mud.

The faith of those involved in funding and dedicating memorials in those early years was enormous. The site resembled a waste ground where, apart from thousand of tree shelters out of which a thistle was as likely to raise its head as a tree, there seemed to be nothing but mud and rubble. Even the River Tame, in the early years before the wonderful cleaning up operation that restored its waters to purity, added to the gloom by providing a background perfume that was far from pleasantly aromatic. There were many who expected instant transformation of this waste ground and reasonably sized trees but they were far outnumbered by those who had the patience to wait, even if it meant that they themselves would not see their tree reach maturity. The concept that we were creating a gift for future generations to reflect upon and enjoy was one that people could understand even in an age where, thanks to television programmes, gardens appeared to be created in an instant. But trees are different; plant them small and leave them undisturbed and they will become a thing of beauty that will still be giving pleasure in one hundred years or, in a few cases, one thousand. Plant them as semi-mature tall trees and the cost of purchase will be so much higher as their life expectancy will be so much lower. Frankly, the poor condition of the soil at the Arboretum did not justify our planting expensive trees.

The Great War

It came as no surprise that the majority of those involved with the Arboretum's plots had links to the Second World War and after. An ambitious plan to involve the Western Front Association through the creation of a trench and groves alongside the 'no-man's land' that followed the line of the large gas-pipe line under the Arboretum came to nothing, meaning that we were in danger of not recalling the sacrifice of those who took part in the Great War. Then, through one of the Far East Prisoners of War, Jack Plant, we gained an opportunity to remember Gallipoli. Jack had been befriended by a Turkish expat, Nadir Imanoglu, who acted as his volunteer chauffeur whenever Jack wished to visit the site. Nadir had never been to Gallipoli but after several conversations with me decided both to visit the peninsula and to undertake to design, fund and create a Gallipoli memorial at the Arboretum. For him, a Turk, to do this in tribute, as it would be seen, to the British and Commonwealth personnel who had died on the peninsula, recalled some wonderful words spoken by Kemal Ataturk, the founder of modern Turkey, and hero of Gallipoli:

Those heroes who shed their blood on the land of a distant country, here you lie on the soil of a friendly nation. Sleep in peace and tranquillity. You lie side by side with the Mehemetciks [equivalent of 'Tommies'] and in each others arms. You, the mothers who sent your sons to war from faraway countries, wipe away your tears. Your sons are in our bosom. They are in peace and they will sleep in peace. After giving their lives on this soil they have become our sons as well.

This should be read in parallel with Rupert Brooke's most famous sonnet:

> If I should die, think only this of me:
> That there's some corner of a foreign field
> That is for ever England ...

It provides a feeling of calm and peace and the belief that, in McNeice's words, 'For all the spite and hatred and betrayal, men had the nobler qualities of men'; and that, in the end, maybe the far and distant end, 'all will be well'. We may not live to see it but while the trees grow we can hope.

The Far East

The skeletons moved slowly, shuffling toward where the taxiing plane was coming to a halt. When it finally did so they grouped below the steps and waited for the passengers to descend. The first one to come towards them was a lady, the first English woman they had seen for four years. Ignoring their pitiful nakedness she put her arms around them. They never forgot that: it was love at first sight. She was Lady Edwina Mount batten and they were survivors of the Sumatra Railway. The date was 16 September 1945. It remained etched in the minds of those who watched as this beautiful lady dressed in a military uniform and wearing a head scarf approached them. Jack Plant, one of those near naked men, later recorded the moment in a poem dedicated to Edwina Mountbatten:

> The first that we knew was the buzz of a light propeller
> The second the glint of equatorial un on the wings
> We stood bemused, t'was small to deliver ton-size packs
> Or to lift half-naked skeletons from this hell-hole.
>
> It taxied to a halt, spluttered and stopped
> She stepped out, ye t'was female, what should we do
> It wore a skirt and had a hair do
> We dropped our hands the better to hide our smalls,
> Her stride was purposeful but said, 'no don't run away'.
>
> She was in khaki, not bad looking, spoke like you and me
> 'How long have you been here? We knew nothing of a railway.'
> She held out a hand, shook ours vigorously

Conversation burst forth as between old friends
Easy as an old boot, ten to the dozen.

With determination she headed for the nearest billet, stood at a doorway,
Seeing the misery a tear came, she brushed it away as though ashamed
'My husband will soon have you out of here on your way home'
Spoken with authority, t'was what we wanted to hear.

Shook hands again and turned towards the plane ·
The lady had risked her well-being, maybe her life,
We who had nothing before, now had confidence
And just a spark of happiness,
Engine spluttered into life, she waved and was gone
We never saw her again
The lady who cared.

It was not great poetry but it sums up a moment of great poignancy far better than any reporter could have done. Fifty years later, those who are bemused at the effect that a brief visit by Diana, Princess of Wales, used to have on deprived communities or the suffering, might find a precedent in the aura of hope and joy that Edwina Mountbatten brought to those desperate men of the Sumatra Railway.

When the story of the suffering of the Far East Prisoners of War in World War Two is told it is the deprivations endured during the construction of the notorious Burma Railway that is recounted; that, and the suffering in Changi Jail. Few even know that a similar railway was built on the Indonesian island of Sumatra: a 140 mile track from Padang to Pakanburu through equatorial rainforest that had to be cleared by hand. To undertake this work some 5,000 allied Prisoners of War were ferried from Malaya to Sumatra where they were reinforced by 30,000 'romushas' or local labourers. By the end of their work, this completed railway, which was never used, had cost the lives of 700 POWs and 25,000 romushas. The much longer 'Burma Railway', over 415 kilometres including the famous Bridge on the River Kwai was built at a cost of around 16,000 allied lives. Through Jack's efforts those who had laboured as hard and suffered as much building the smaller line would achieve equal recognition at the Arboretum.

Although it was determined from the start of the arboretum that there should be a memorial to those who had served and suffered in the Far East, the original concept was a small wood. Donations for trees in this wood began to be received almost as soon as the project was made public and, very soon, sufficient progress had been made with the Appeal to consider what might be a more appropriate way to acknowledge this very special group.

During a meeting held to discuss the creation of a museum at Three Pagodas Pass on the Burma Railway I raised the possibility of having some of the rails shipped to Britain. The British Military Attaché in Bangkok expressed himself willing to act as an intermediary and to organise the shipment of the rails to the docks, provided the Arboretum could find a way to transport them to UK. It took another two years to obtain a length of rail together with the sleepers and spikes. That delay was no bad thing. In the intervening years the Arboretum design had grown sufficiently to set aside an area for the railway track and to convince FEPOWs across the nation that the site would be an appropriate one at which to tell their story. The FEPOWs themselves demanded, quite rightly, to be involved and informed at every step. They were a remarkable group. Each one exuded a air of quiet dignity and gave the impression of having been into the furnace and emerged with a sliver of steel running the length of his spine. One knew, without their even talking about their experiences, that they had endured much and come through a savage test; without demanding it they commanded respect.

Although few did talk about their experiences one of them, Fred Seiker, a Dutchman who came to live in the UK immediately upon his release, painted pictures of what he had seen. His stark, simple and haunting images became a permanent display in the Visitor Centre and informed better than a thousand words those who wished to know more about a FEPOW's life. Fred's own description of two of his paintings might suffice to give a glimpse of what he and others had to endure:

Picture 13. Tropical Ulcer. The most dreaded of all sores. The slightest scratch could start this awful rotting disease. Bamboo wound usually turned into a spreading rotting ulcer. In the absence of any medication, the only remedy (although only temporary) to keep the wound clean was to scrape the rotting flesh away with a sharpened spoon! Many a leg amputation was carried out as a result of tropical ulcers.

Picture 15. Nurse in River Incident. This surely must count as one of the most loathsome tortures a human being could contrive. A POW would be ordered by a guard into the river where so called Japanese 'nurses' were bathing in the nude. The victim would be forced to wash one of the nurse's backs watched by the guard. The POW would be called back to the river bank upon which the 'nurses' would make lewd gestures. If the POW then showed even the slightest sign of sexual excitement, the guard would hit his penis hard with a thin pliable bamboo. The extreme pain and mental humiliation for the POW was total. It is known that the victims of this torture received lifelong physical damage and mental anguish.

With the track and sleepers ready to be moved from Thailand, the organisation of its shipping to the UK was the next obstacle. Here, as so often, serendipity played its part. An old friend of mine, Admiral Sir Alan West, had recently been appointed Commander-in-Chief Fleet and he was able to tell me that HMS *Northumberland* would not only be visiting Bangkok shortly but would be delighted to transport the rails back to Devonport. The Ministry of Defence were also prepared to transport the thirty-metre length of track from the West Country to the Arboretum.

So it was that on 7 January 2001 a group of FEPOWs gathered on the flight deck of HMS *Northumberland* to be reunited with the railway that they had suffered so much to construct. It was an emotional moment. Roy Blacker from Plympton, Tom Webber from Plymouth and Steve Cairns from Somerset were among those who bravely gave interviews before sitting down beside the tracks in silence to reflect on their memories that the sight of the sleepers and rails brought flooding back.

"Looking at it now," said 83 year old Roy," I don't see rail or sleepers. I think of all my mates that were left behind. They were young lads – 23 or 24 years of age – young happy lads. You have never seen a finer set of men. We worked together and suffered together. I knew today wouldn't be easy. We suffered so much and I lost a lot of friends. No one can understand, and that is why we need this memorial so that it never happens again."

The next day the rails and sleepers set out on their journey to the Arboretum where a large contingent of FEPOWs and their families had gathered to welcome them to the site. Railtrack had kindly supplied some twenty old wooden sleepers which would support the ones from Thailand so that they were kept clear of the ground. Nevertheless, there was concern that these old, untreated timbers would degenerate rapidly in the English climate. We sought professional advice only to be told that if they had managed to survive sixty years in the jungle they should manage anything that the British weather might throw at them. Nevertheless, it was important that they were regularly monitored. No such concerns arose over the rails which looked to be in excellent condition. When the Japanese decided to build the railway they used local timber for the sleepers but ripped up railway lines in China for which they had no use themselves to provide the rails. This then raised the intriguing question as to where the rails might have been manufactured in the first place. One of the Friends, Maynard Scott, set himself the task of finding out, a quest in which he was assisted, appropriately, by members of the Birmingham Branch of the FEPOW Association. Starting with the legends 'BV&Co 1904' and 'IV MR 60 LBS' which could just be discerned on one of the rails, Maynard found that they had been made by Bolckow, Vaughan & Co., a company that had been based at Middlesborough. Although their actual journey from the North East to the Far East could not be traced, the irony that it was

The Prime Minister, John Major, launches the National Memorial Arboretum Appeal, flanked by (*left to right*) Sir Peter Ramsbotham, Chairman, World Memorial Fund, Lord Barber of Tewkesbury, Chairman, The National Forest and Sir Colin Corness, Chairman of Redland Aggregates. November 1994. *The National Forest*

A thousand years ahead of it: the barren site of the National Memorial Arboretum, waterlogged and treeless before landscaping began in 1997. *NMA*

The lone and level wastes: the site for the Army 'Parade' after ripping but before the infantry regiment plots were planted. *NMA*

The Visitor Centre entrance ahead of the formal opening, showing Architype's curved wooden roof, the tall 'Gallery' and the outside of the cloisters to the left. *Architype*

The tall, pillared 'Millennium Chapel of Peace and Forgiveness' showing its classic ancient Greek temple lines, redolent of the religious buildings where Christianity was first preached two thousand years ago. *Architype*

The Chapel in 2007 looking across the cloister through the War Widows' Rose Garden. *Driftwood*

'The Storyteller', a magical piece of work by the Essex Woodcarvers based around their family members. The little boy on the right is leaning over to catch a carved snail, which was what he was doing when his grandmother sketched him. *Driftwood*

The Chapel, facing the altar with the Commonwealth War Graves Sword of Sacrifice in the centre and the two thieves' crosses on either side. The altar is draped with the 'Tree of Life' frontal while a number of Veterans' Associations standards have been laid up on the left. *Driftwood*

'The Friends' at work over a weekend planting and tying in a hedge. *NMA*

Very few semi-mature trees were planted. Those that were, required much more expensive equipment and expertise than the smaller saplings, making them unaffordable for most donors. Here Barry Jones, the Head Groundsman (*back to camera*) supervises the planting of one such tree. *Driftwood*

The DEMS and Maritime RA Bofors Gun at the head of Pedestal Avenue with the Merchant Navy 'Convoy' beyond. *Driftwood*

A path through 'The Convoy' showing the oaks, representing merchant ships lost in the Second World War, growing sturdily. At the far end is a plinth listing the losses of just one shipping company. *Driftwood*

The pond and waterfall in the Royal Artillery plot. *NMA*

The RAF Boy Entrants
memorial and plinths
listing the air stations
where they trained between
1934 and 1965. The same
four-bladed propeller motif,
but in hedging, can be seen
at the RAF Halton
Apprentices plot. *Driftwood*

The life-size 49 Division Polar Bear, the first sculpture on the site and the first work undertaken by the Essex Woodcarvers. The circular brick base, a difficult construction job, was undertaken by students from Burton-on-Trent Technical College. *NMA*

The RAF Regiment's plot in winter with the FEPOW Museum behind. *NMA*

A stretch of the notorious 'Burma Railway' shipped back from Thailand to form the central feature of the FEPOW Plot. Ironically, the rails were manufactured in England for a railway in China from where they were ripped up for use on the death track. *NMA*

The dedication of the Berlin Airlift Memorial with the golden eagle soaring above the Association's air-lane symbol. *NMA*

Bevin Boys assembling by their standard prior to marching past on National Service Veterans' Day 2006. *Driftwood*

The Mercian Wood, a planting of native deciduous trees dedicated to individuals. *NMA*

The Irish Ash Grove memorial plinth within its circle of boulders, each brought over from a county within Ulster. *NMA*

The ATS Ack Ack plot on the day of its dedication. *Driftwood*

The sculpture of a lifeboat man, carved on site, dominates the RNLI plot created through the enthusiasm of the Tamworth Branch of the RNLI, the furthest inland. *Driftwood*

The rising sun lights up the lonely figure of Private Andrew Burden tied and blindfolded in front of the stakes on which the names of all those 'Shot at Dawn' are recorded; in front, the six cypresses represent the firing squad, most of whom abhorred the task they had been ordered to perform. *NMA*

A small visitor on a day she will remember, handing a posy to Her Majesty the Queen during her Millennium Visit to the Arboretum. *NMA*

The great courtyard of the Armed Force Memorial on top of its tumulus with the obelisk directing attention skyward. On the curved walls are recorded the names of all Service and Merchant Navy personnel killed on active service since the end of the Second World War. *Driftwood*

'The Pity of War' – a dying 'warrior' is carried away reverently by his colleagues while an anguished mother and child look on. The scene does not represent any particular incident or campaign but depicts both the sorrow and the dignity experienced in conflict. *Driftwood*

British-manufactured rails that the prisoners had laid was not lost, but neither was the joy, if inanimate objects can have a soul, of their return to the country that gave them birth a century earlier. May they lie in peace.

A short time later Jack Plant created a replica length of the Sumatra Railway to lie at right angles to the Burma track. He had charmed, cajoled and persuaded Railtrack and Forest Enterprise to provide him with track and sleepers and had also managed to get a well designed plinth built with donated tricks and cast bronze plaques to tell the story.

Most of the men who were captured by the Japanese in Singapore were interned in the prison at Changi where the crowded and insanitary conditions soon led to a high death rate. When the dead were removed for burial they were carried to their graves with little ceremony. To counter this unfeeling attitude Captain Pickersgill and the men of 18 Div RE designed and built a lych gate that would stand four square on the route to the cemetery and through which everybody destined for burial would pass. The gates were built from local timber and in each corner, up in the eves, Sergeant Mercer of 560 Coy RE carved the four symbols of the nations that make up the United Kingdom, a rose, a daffodil a thistle and a shamrock. The gates remained at Changi until the British withdrawal from the Far East when they were shipped to and rebuilt at Bassingbourn Barracks near Cambridge, an RE training centre whose East Anglian location meant it was in the region where many of the Regiments captured at Singapore were based. In time the role of the barracks changed and its Commanding Officer decided that there might be a more appropriate site for the Changi gates. The local branch of COFEPOW (Children of Far East Prisoners of War), led by that association's founder, Carol Cooper, suggested that the NMA might be the most appropriate location. The transfer was arranged following a most moving service at Bassingbourn, at which Terry Waite, himself the victim of many years of unjust captivity, spoke most eloquently.

The rededication at the site had been planned for 15 February 2004, the anniversary of the fall of Singapore, but it was brought forward one week so that the men of 39 Engineering Regiment who had restored and re-erected the gate, and who were leaving for Gibraltar on 13 February could attend.

Carol Cooper and her colleagues, like the Arboretum, had for some years been nursing an ambition to create a small museum in tribute to their parents and all who had been imprisoned in the Far East. Two issues had delayed their progress: the location and the funding. Now, with the Arboretum taking shape the location became apparent and we were united in the idea that the NMA with its central location and growing reputation would be a fitting place for the museum. That left funding which, as with so many Arboretum projects began at zero. However, we did have a building design, based on one of the large village huts that can be seen in Thailand, and an idea of costs. Moreover, from the fall of Singapore on 15 February 1942, when most of the prisoners were captured, to the end of the war on 15 August 1945 lay 1188 days; our appeal began in mid February 2002 with the aim of opening the museum on 15 August 2005. Each day could be linked to one of those eleven hundred and so we asked people to sponsor a day, or even an hour of captivity. Many did, linking their gift with some poignant memory such as the date on which their loved one had succumbed to disease, malnutrition or torture. This idea appealed particularly to Carol Cooper whose own father, William Smith, had sailed for the Far East on his and her mother's 26th birthday just before Carol herself was two. They received no letters from him after his capture and he received none from her mother. All Mrs Smith heard was a note from the War Office in 1943 saying that he was a prisoner and another in October 1945 saying that he had died. Later Carol found out that he had written a diary in which he recorded his 14 months spent in Changi Jail before he, along with 7,000 others, was shipped, crammed into trucks up to work on the railway. After 36 hours without food or water during which many of them died they were forced to march 240 miles in monsoon conditions from camp to camp.

William Smith's diary ended on 8 December 1943, nine days before he died from the combined effects of malaria, dysentery, malnutrition and cardiac beri beri. The discovery of his diary and a trip to Thailand in 1996 led to Carol starting COFEPOW. Her commitment to the memory of the father she never knew has given many others a similar opportunity to pay tribute to their own long lost parents. But COFEPOW was achieving more than that; it had taken up the message latent in the FEPOW prayer, quoted earlier, and indicated its willingness to carry the torch on for at least another generation.

As the museum appeal was progressing, the Millennium Commission announced that it had found some more money. It sounded as if one of the staff had opened a bottom drawer and found it full of fivers, but this was, in fact, money set aside for projects which had not come to fruition. Those projects that needed further funds to consolidate or develop their sites were invited to apply for support with a list of ideas, although it was stressed there was not sufficient funding to go around, and only one suggestion at the most was likely to be supported. We came up with eight ideas including landscaping the front of the site, improving the car park, providing a shelter near Shot at Dawn, a shelter and information centre at the Irish Ash Grove and the FEPOW Museum. We were told that we would be visited by a member of staff who could spend no more than an hour on site and would, if she felt minded, recommend just one of our list. We got her back in her car with one minute to spare and then were most pleasantly surprised to be told several weeks later that all our requests would be met. The FEPOW museum was going to happen!

By the time that the Millennium money was made available to enable work to begin I had moved on, but Sir Henry Every and Carol's team worked together to produce what was to be a most well proportioned and appropriate building in which the museum's designer, Chris Hudson, was able to tell the story of the FEPOWs, including Carol's own father, with a clarity which avoided either glossing over or sanitizing the facts, so that the visitor is given a very comprehensive picture of what those who had been captured endured.

The museum fronts on to an L-shaped bank on which the memorials to the Burma and Sumatra railway were placed. In the area enclosed by this bank it had been my intention to place a tribute to the soldiers of General Slim's army who had fought to drive the Japanese out of Burma. The tribute was to be in the form of a tennis court, which would certainly puzzle most visitors. When Slim decided that the time was right to stand fast against the Japanese he ordered two strongholds to be established at the towns of Kohima and Imphal. Much of the fierce hand-to-hand fighting at the former took place across the tennis court that lay in the grounds of the British residence's property.

In slight simplicity I had considered that the FEPOWs and the Burma Star Association represented two parts of the same story: one that began with the Japanese invasions and the Fall of Singapore and ended with the release of the captives after the hard fought struggle by 14th Army and its supporting elements. This was not a whim, for the idea had been based around the title of Slim's own account of the campaign, "Defeat into Victory". What I had wanted to do at the site was to show the triumph of good over evil in a way that could be clearly understood. For this reason I had interwoven the plots for the two organizations with no clear boundary between the FEPOW area and that designated for the Burma Star planted around the Kohima tennis court. Wrong! I wrote to the Chairman of the Burma Star Association, Captain Paddy Vincent, explaining my ideas and saying that: 'To my generation, children at school today, and future generations, the war in the Far East is and will be seen as a continuing campaign. Its low point was the fall of Singapore and the turn of the tide was signified by Kohima.'

Captain Vincent clarified his Association's point of view, writing back that: 'We have the greatest feeling of comradeship and sympathy with them [the FEPOWs] but the Association was established specifically to bind, commemorate and assist those who fought in the Burma Campaign … all bound by the privilege of wearing the Burma Star, (which our friends the FEPOWs, for all our admiration, do not share).'

A redesign and relocation thus proved necessary and in both of these the Burma Star Association members played a full and energetic part, in the layout of their plot, the choice of plants and the provision of voluntary labour to manure and prepare the ground. We then had different views as to the choice of plants; I wanted to use the planting as an opportunity to extend the range of plants on display to the visitor and to encourage them to think of the flora in the Far East by planting trees and shrubs redolent of the campaign area, while the Association, as their Vice Chairman, Hedley Vinall, explained, 'still prefer our commemoration to be portrayed by a small British wood, it would seem to be more appropriate for our memorial than using the tree and plants experienced out East which did not exactly endear themselves to us when we were over there!'

This antipathy of the FEPOWs to even the plants that they had come into contact with should not have taken me by surprise, but it was a fiercely held view. Both organizations were insistent that, whatever the final selection of plants turned out to be, none with the word '*japonica*' as part of their descriptive should come anywhere near their plots. There was, however, one tree with whose presence we were in full agreement. The Burma Star veterans had all emphasized how reliant they had been on air drops for their supplies and wanted a way in which to show this. I suggested the planting of *Davidia involucrata*, the Dove tree, whose beautiful large white bracts could be suggestive of parachutes. We agreed on that. Elsewhere around the world it may be referred to as the handkerchief tree, at the Arboretum it became the parachute tree.

It was never our business to propose forgiveness and reconciliation to a generation which had endured so much and lived so long. They had a tough enough task coping with the traumas that tortured their bodies and souls on a daily basis to be called upon by the more fortunate to pick up the added burden of forgiveness. But for some it was a burden they were prepared to shoulder. The President of the FEPOW Association was the Revd Ray Rossiter who, because of the demands of his faith, not only had to find his own path to forgiveness, but had also to serve and minister to comrades whom he knew would never tread that road with him. It says much for Ray's personality that he had been invited to be the FEPOW's President, but he was a man who could preach, with a voice like gravel flowing through treacle, yet never lecture. His address at the dedication of the Burma Railway Plot was an uplifting one for it spoke to us all of the indomitable spirit of men.

One other man who had set his hand to plough a furrow of forgiveness through fields of conflict was Philip Malins, a veteran of the Burma Campaign in which he had been awarded the Military Cross. Philip was the co-founder of the International Friendship And Reconciliation Trust and was involved with bringing about peace and reconciliation in both Germany and Japan. He was also a member of the team that worked so tirelessly to win compensation for all the FEPOWs, so his task of reconciliation won for many a just although tardy settlement. Philip wanted to create a plot that would celebrate forgiveness. The obvious place for this was with the UN Spiral which was, luckily, some way away from the Far East Campaign plots. Here we could introduce plants of Japanese origin, especially and delightfully many species of flowering cherry. Philip's Grove of International Friendship also had space for trees linked to bombed cities such as Dresden, Coventry and Hiroshima, emphasizing a bond created by mutual suffering.

The Grove was dedicated by The Right Reverend Colin Bennetts, Bishop of Coventry, on 15 August 2001, the first anniversary in the new millennium of the end of the second world war. Together the Bishop and the Japanese Ambassador, HE Sadayuki Hayashi, planted two trees. Another three were planted on behalf of the citizens of the war-torn island of Okinawa. If any plot at the Arboretum symbolized the desire for peace and reconciliation between nations this was the one.

CHAPTER FIVE

Wreaths of Empire: Cold War, Conflicts and the End of Empire

Happy was your death. You paid for your Fatherland the common debt that all men owe to Nature. So this fabric is reared, and the letters inscribed upon it, as an eternal testimony of your valour. Those who look upon your monument will never cease to recount your deeds in words of gratitude. So instead of the mortality of human life you have obtained immortality.

Cicero, *Philippic XIV*

One of my earliest recollections of listening to the radio was in a flat at Weymouth overlooking the Bay, where my father's ship HMS *Indefatigable*, an aircraft carrier, was anchored for Christmas. The news I was listening to came from Cyprus where it was reported crowds had gathered and were shouting anti-British slogans. That is precisely the words that I thought they were using and I can remember walking onto the fire escape and shouting, 'Anti-British slogans' neither knowing what that meant or why they should be on the lips of the crowd.

What I did know is that there were service men and women in Cyprus, Germany, Kenya, Malaya and many other areas of the world. I knew this because every Sunday lunchtime we sat down to listen to 'Forces Favourites' which was followed, I believe, by the totally incomprehensible Goon Show and later by the far easier to understand 'Navy Lark' with which, because of my father, I felt a bond. Concepts such as Commonwealth and Empire meant very little to me until I became interested in stamps and until my father's last sea appointment.

Born in 1947, I knew nothing of the war years, and its after effects were only apparent in the rationing of sweets. Other issues, such as the 'Iron Curtain', the establishment of the State of Israel and the granting of independence to erstwhile colonies meant little until HMS *Bermuda*, a Colony Class Cruiser in which my father was serving, spent her last commission sailing around the globe to attend Independence Ceremonies. Many of those Ceremonies, amicable at the time, had come about after years of tension and conflict. The incidents to which I had listened on the news with their reports of EOKA terrorists, the Mau Mau, and Chinese Communists had all involved loss of life among a generation which had already given many of its own in the Second World War. Yet my generation were born into a half century of conflict, in every year of which, apart from 1966, British Service personnel, were to lose their lives on active duty.

In my early years the veracity of Churchill's statement that an iron curtain had descended over eastern Europe was proven by the decision of the Soviet Union to blockade West Berlin, leaving only three narrow air corridors by which to move in food, fuel and support. For fifteen months the two million inhabitants of the city were kept alive and free by an 'air bridge' along which Royal Air Force and Allied airmen flew in almost two and a half million tons of supplies and returned with thousands of elderly and sick Berliners. In the face of such unchallengeable resolve the Soviet Union had no option but to admit defeat and lift the blockade, which they did on 12 May 1949. It was a victory won through much courage, great skill, adamantine resolve and no little loss. Seventy Allied aircrew together with eight German civilians died during the operation. As with so many operations where people live in close proximity to danger and each other, those who took part formed an Association to keep the memories of their achievements alive and to act as a support service for their former comrades. The British Berlin Airlift Association's badge recalls their work. It consists of three parallel, curved vertical lines, representing the air lanes into Berlin, surmounted by an eagle. When they approached the Arboretum to discuss establishing a tribute on the site it seemed obvious that their badge offered us an opportunity to unite the talents of Andy de Comyn and the Essex Woodcarvers. Together they designed a twelve foot concrete plinth, shaped like the air lane badge, surmounted by a wooden golden eagle, which they then proceeded to deliver for erection between the car park and the entrance to the Arboretum, where every visitor would walk past it. Some initial problems with the base were overcome and Andy worked out a way to prevent the surface of the structure from cracking, while the eagle was the acme of the woodcarvers' art. Peter and his team took hundreds of photographs of a female eagle in captivity and spent weeks studying the bird's anatomy so that their life-size spread-winged bird would be exact in every detail. It was a shame to have to raise her up where her fine lines could not be studied in detail, but once in place she gave a soaring greeting to every visitor to the Arboretum. On one side of the plinth an Avenue of thirty-nine cherry trees was planted in memory of each of the British and Commonwealth airmen who had been lost in the airlift. For a moment lime trees had been considered as a link with the famous Berlin Avenue, the *Unter den Linden*, but they had been dismissed as needing too much room. The cherries would be in blossom on the anniversary of the lifting of the blockade and would serve as a reminder that fresh food had to be delivered to the besieged citizens as well as fuel and other necessities. Two plinths between the memorial and the trees listed the names of those lost and told the story of the airlift.

Positioned where it was, the obvious place at which to gather for the dedication of the Berlin Airlift Memorial was the car park. Unfortunately, this had not been completed at the time that it was decided to hold the dedication here. The Arboretum never failed to deliver an event when planned but this was the closet we got to failure. During the morning of the dedication, Paul Harrington and his team continued to bulldoze and spread hardcore into place, working to a deadline that it seemed impossible for them to meet. As the guests arrived, the heavy machinery departed, giving the team just enough time to lay out the chairs on the well rolled surface before the Service began. It went well. The high point was when Dennis Sanders released a flock of white doves as the congregation stood in silent remembrance. Instead of rising vertically, the doves flew down the open aisle level with the crowd, turned, flew back and then climbed away homeward, leaving many tearful face behind them.

The Korean War was another campaign that the British fought in miserable conditions against a fanatical foe who treated its captives with a contempt similar to that experienced by the FEPOWs of the second world war, some of whom were to find themselves prisoners a second time in a fairly short service career. One of those who was captured and who was to show his mettle in the camps was Captain Anthony Farrar-Hockley, who on return to active service rose to the rank of General and was now the Senior Patron of the British Korean Veterans' Association (BKVA). Here, at the Arboretum he had much to be proud of in what had been achieved in the name of the Association by local volunteers.

Most of the projects at the Arboretum started with the idea of a tree bearing a label. As support grew so the number of trees desired increased and the scale of the 'label' grew. It was much the same with the BKVA; we started with the idea of planting some trees dedicated to individuals who had served in Korea and developed this into a circular garden of red and blue flowers and shrubs planted to form a 'yin yang', the Korean symbol of good luck, and situated on the bank at the end of Giffard Avenue where it was clearly visible for those walking along its length.

Preparing the garden was a nightmare, of which guarding against attack by rabbits was just one element but one which those who had repelled wave after wave of Communist Chinese were determined to overcome. The hardest task was creating a garden on a bank that consisted of stone and dust with no humus, no structure and a tolerance for weeds which it refused to expand to include flowers and shrubs. The BKVA fought on, bringing in supplies of manure and reinforcements armed with spades. They dug for and achieved victory.

Above the 'yin yang' at the top of the ridge four massive boulders were placed to represent the four years that the war lasted and on each of these were recorded the units taking part in that year. On either side trees native to Korea, including the wonderful blue Korean pine, *Pinus koraiensis*, were planted to form a link with that peninsula. Week after week the local members of the BKVA toiled at their plot until, with their numbers diminishing, they were forced to withdraw and allow the 'yin yang' to return to grass. However, their planting around the spot meant that the area would grow as one with very special links to the Far East.

*   *   *

Between 1947 and 1960 the majority of the young men of Great Britain underwent a rite of passage that was to last over one year and to transport them from boyhood to adulthood. Although many and various events took place during that time the initiation ceremony inevitably began with the ceremonial haircut, the issue of ill-fitting and scratchy garments, and the provision of ill-fitting and dull boots which required a magic potion of spit, warmed teaspoons and polish to shine up; all this in preparation for the main initiating event which involved strange, ancient processions around a parade ground while being shouted at by junior NCOs who used the f-word as every conceivable part of speech including pronoun, preposition and conjunction. Nights were spent either in the novitiates' long-hut or 'barrack-room' or whiled away in late-night vigils known as guard duty. This was National Service, and after their initiation many went on to serve with distinction both at home and abroad. At one time over half of the strength of Infantry Regiments in Korea consisted of these short-term servicemen. They fought hard and won the respect of the regulars, and not only in Korea; wherever the services were deployed National Servicemen could be found enduring the rough and enjoying the smooth. They were present in Palestine and at the debacle that was Suez, both conflicts which were to have their own memorials at the NMA, and in Aden, Malaya and in Africa, National Servicemen served and died. As most of the youth of Britain was involved, many of those who were to become the most famous names of their generation endured the common experience. They included football stars like the Charlton brothers; entertainers such as Ronnie Corbett and Bob Monkhouse; broadcasters like Michael Parkinson; DJs like Jimmy Saville; writers such as Auberon Waugh and Leslie Thomas; and politicians such as Tam Dalyell and Michael

Heseltine. Some stayed on after their time was up, with Field Marshals the Lord Vincent and Sir John Chapple, reaching the highest rank of all. It is true that for many the experience was unpleasing, dull and seen as a waste of time, but it did unite a generation in peace through a common experience that was normally only the preserve of wartime. The conflicts of their time claimed the lives of 395 of them; many more died in activities directly linked to these conflicts such as training accidents, crashes and weapon discharges. The names of these are recorded on the Armed Forces Memorial in whose shadow lies the tribute erected by the National Service Veterans themselves and before which they parade in their thousands every June. Most of them wear the unofficial National Service Medal created by Bob Van Mook, the managing director of Award Productions, who gave considerable support to the building of the National Service Memorial, four thin shafts of grey surmounted by a silver crown, and continues to give thousands of pounds from the sale of the medal towards the work of The Royal British Legion. The determination to create the memorial as a tribute to some two million men and to have a National Service Sunday was spearheaded by a very determined gentleman, Gerald Rose, who has ensured that on the nearest Sunday to 23 June every year, several thousands of ex-National Servicemen and their families enjoy a day of celebration and refection at the Arboretum. As Gerald included in his vision the war years of compulsory enlistment it is also an occasion when veteran Bevin Boys, the men who were conscripted into the mines during the war, also have a chance to parade with pride; their march past, which takes in their own plot as well as the National Service Memorial, is the most warmly applauded of them all.

*   *   *

National Service was well past by the time Britain began what was to be the nation's longest single conflict in modern times – the 'Troubles' in Northern Ireland. Gunner Robert Curtis, a twenty year old member of the Royal Artillery was shot by an IRA sniper in North Belfast on 6 February 1971; Lance Bombardier Stephen Restorick was shot and killed at a checkpoint on 12 February 1997. In the intervening years another 717 service men and women died on active duty both in Northern Ireland and in related incidents on mainland Britain. For a while no record was kept or tribute planned for these victims of a domestic conflict. And it might never have been were it not for a campaign by one newspaper, *The Daily Telegraph*, and one mother, Mrs Rita Restorick.

Rita Restorick's quest seemed to be not solely for justice, but neither was it for revenge. What she seemed above all to represent in her mother's grief was the desire to drive home to both politicians and men of violence just how precious and unique a child's life is. Yet she was never unaware of the paradox that the uniqueness of her son Stephen was one shared by every mother of every person killed in the euphemistically named 'Troubles'. Her book about Stephen, *Death of a Soldier*, could refer to any of over 700 men who were killed in the province. Although the book talks of one, Stephen Restorick, his life, his death, her grief, her response, embraces them all.

Stephen was killed at a checkpoint at Bessbrook on 12 February 1997. He and his colleagues in the Royal Horse Artillery had been in Northern Ireland since Boxing Day 1996. He was twelve days short of his twenty-fourth birthday, on which anniversary would fall the day of his funeral. There were no national plans to pay tribute to him and more than 700 other Service men and women killed in Northern Ireland

Then the *Daily Telegraph* began a campaign to remind the nation of the loss of life that the 'Troubles' had caused. At this time the Arboretum had sketchy plans for recording the names of those listed by the *Daily Telegraph*, but the newspaper's campaign spurred us into action and we proposed planting a tree for each life lost. Lord Brooke, a former Secretary of State for Northern Ireland, liked the idea and raised the subject with both the incumbent Minister and the Northern Ireland Office. Both expressed interest and shortly afterward we began discussions with the latter about the design and whom to include in the memorial.

I had thought it would be a wonderful idea to make the focus of the memorial a cairn of stone brought over from the hexagonal basalt that formed the world famous Giant's Causeway. The National Trust of Northern Ireland were not so enamoured of the idea but, as was so often the case, out of the seed sprung an unexpected tree. The Northern Ireland Office liked our alternative suggestion, which was for a boulder to be brought over from each of the six counties of Ulster. They liked it so much that they organised a geologist, Alan Bell, to seek out, procure and deliver the boulders along with a large central monolith on which words could be carved. Here again occurred a wonderful example of serendipity. Lord Brooke's son, Sebastian, was a sculptor and his father commissioned him to engrave the simple dedicatory lines. The details of the stones are at Appendix D.

As it was our intention to plant a tree for each lost life we needed an enormous plot, for to end up with 746 trees (719 armed forces, 60 Ulster Defence Regiment, 38 for former Royal Ulster Constabulary sub-divisions and 29 for prison officers) we had to plant over two thousand saplings so that two out of three could eventually be thinned, leaving the remainder tall and straight and proud. The species of tree we chose to plant was Ash, linking it to that gently sad Irish song, 'Down by the Ash Grove'. This also gave us an opportunity to introduce a new collection of trees on to the site and seven types of Ash were selected for the planting which was laid out in the form of a gentle curve radiating from the ring of stones. We were not long into the planting of this wood when we began to appreciate why most woodland is planted in straight lines; curves are difficult! But they are more peaceful and reflective. At the front of the grove was planted a crescent of weeping ash, *Fraxinus excelsior* 'Pendula', that would grow to form a backdrop for the stones.

The site large enough to plant this tribute lay above the old silt beds of the gravel pits. This meant that the ash tree of the Ulster Grove would get the best possible start in life. They throve, 'nursed' by protective willow and poplar, and we lost not a single tree.

We were very lucky in the funding of the project because, in addition to the Regiments in which most of those being remembered had served, contributions were made by the Northern Ireland Office, Trusts, Sponsors and individuals. The Government and Northern Ireland Office were anxious to complete the project once started, and an early visit of inspection by a serving Colonel had reported back unfavourably on the site's development. As was often the case, the time taken to establish trees and paths was not fully understood nor was the impracticality of wishing to see a mature site created instantly with young trees which, by definition, are being grown for the future. Others, however, felt much more positive. Both the RUC, shortly to become the Police Service of Northern Ireland, and the Province's Prison Service, wanted the lost lives of their members to be remembered at the site. For the former we planted a dedicatory Avenue with a tree for each Police District; the latter had a tree for each Officer killed. All this was overseen with calm authority by Alan Tipping from the Northern Ireland Office who, it appeared, was never phased by the early criticisms and thus a great ally to have.

The memorial stones, weighing between five and twelve tonnes, arrived on a sodden winter day on board two of the largest vehicles ever to enter the Arboretum. Venturing onto soggy silt beds was not a good idea and the lead lorry was soon axle deep in mud. Luckily, once the stones were lifted off the lorries could move away. Strangely, as soon as the circle of stones was in place they looked as if they had been there a millennium or more and so gave the spot a dignity and significance that belied its age.

On 23 September 2003 Alan organised for the Secretary of State for Northern Ireland, the Rt Hon Paul Murphy MP, the Minister of State, Jane Kennedy MP, the Chief Constable, Hugh Orde and Lieutenant General Trousdell, the GOC, to attend the official opening. The Service was conducted jointly by the four heads of the main Northern Irish Churches and the sun shone on the hundreds of relatives gathered at the Grove. One of the highlights was the reading of the poem written by Lance Bombardier Steven Cummins, who was killed in County Londonderry on 8 March 1989, and which has since become one of the nation's favourites:

Do not stand at my grave and weep;
I am not there, I do not sleep.
I am a thousand winds that blow.
I am the diamond glint on snow.
I am the sunlight on ripened grain.

I am the gentle autumn rain.
When you awaken in the morning's hush
I am the swift uplifting rush
Of quiet bird in circled flight.
I am the soft star that shines at night.
Do not stand at my grave and cry;
I am not there I did not die.

As poignant, although less well known, were the words from *The UDR Soldier* by John Potter:

As poppy petals gently fall
Remember us who gave our all
Not in the mud of foreign lands
Nor buried in the desert sands.

In Ulster field and farm and town
Fermanagh's lanes or drumlin'd Down
We died that violent death should cease
And Ulstermen might live in peace.

Amen to that. Since the dedication of the Ash Grove the sad duty of planting another tree there has not arisen. May it never do so.

Sadly, there was one new plot to which trees were having to be added while this book was being written – those who were dying in the conflicts in Iraq and Afghanistan. The second Iraq war was the first major campaign involving British Forces that had taken place since the Arboretum had been opened and we were concerned that our response should be an appropriate one. Arboriculturally there was one very obvious tree to plant, a weeping willow, whose appropriateness could be interpreted at several levels. *Salix Babylonica*, the Babylon Willow, gained its name from that most passionate expression of homesickness and despair that is voiced in Psalm 137 which bemoans the exile of the Jews on the banks of the Tigris so many miles from their own city, Jerusalem.

The psalm was turned into a moving poem by Byron and later put to a more modern tune sung by, among others, Joan Baez:

We sat down and wept by the waters
Of Babel, and thought of the day
When our foe, in the hue of his slaughters!
Made Salem's high places his prey:

On the willow that harp is suspended,
O, Salem! Its sound should be free;
And the hour when thy glories were ended
But left me that token of thee;

As the death toll from Iraq increased so we used the willow as another symbol of grief and remembrance which allowed us to pay tribute in a way we might not otherwise have found possible.

As our Millennium Chapel had been built of wood it was not possible for us to allow the burning of memorial candles within the chapel by those who might wish to remember a life in this way. However, I had been very taken in the Middle East by how certain trees, often on the outskirts of villages, had small pieces of cloth tied to them usually to mark a wish made at the spot. We combined these two ideas in our weeping willow and tied a small strip of white cloth to its branches every time a British soldier was reported killed. Later we planted a line of willows along the Darbyshire Ditch, trees for those who had lost their lives. Our fervent prayers were that it would be a very short line.

The loss of life in areas of conflict from Berlin to Borneo, from Cyprus to South Georgia and in every year bar one since 1946 meant that some 16,000 British service men and women had been killed on active service in the latter part of the twentieth century and beyond, yet had no central memorial to their sacrifice.

Then, in November 2000 the Secretary of State for Defence, The Rt Hon Geoff Hoon MP, announced in the House of Commons that a memorial would be constructed to pay tribute to those members of the Armed Forces who had lost their lives on active service since the end of the Second World War. He also stated that the memorial would be in London. Alerted to this, we began a campaign to change the location to the NMA. This was more than just desirable, our whole future depended on it. For if the most significant memorial to be raised in the country since the great memorials linked to the losses incurred between 1939 and 1945 was not to be at the Arboretum then our whole claim to be the nation's focus for remembrance would have been swept aside. I contacted the Armed Forces Memorial project officer, Lt Col Richard Callender, and invited him to come and see us.

In early 2001 David Puttnam and I called on the Minister for Veterans Affairs, Dr Lewis Mooney, and asked for his support for the new memorial to be built at the NMA. He, as Ministers do, listened sympathetically and sent us on our way with words of encouraging non-commitedness. Richard Callender's visit took place later that month after which he wrote: 'We briefly touched on the question of the possibility of siting the proposed post WW2 memorial at the Arboreum ... However, no decision has yet been made on siting as the Secretary of State has stated that he want it in Central London.'

We continued lobbying, stating that the new memorial, if sited in central London would act as an alternative venue to the Cenotaph for crowds on 11 November, as memories of the two world wars fade to be replaced by those for whom later conflicts are more significant We also emphasised that our site was a large one entirely devoted to remembrance, including the presence of a chapel dedicated for this purpose, unlike any similar spot in London; what is more, we had the acreage and it would not have to be purchased at commercial rates. We were also easier to reach for the majority of our countrymen, with no massive parking charges. Our trump card, we felt, was our ability to handle educational tours any day of the year, under the direction of our new Education Officer, ex-Head Teacher Tony Critchley. In mid-July, Major General Christopher Elliott and John Sinfield, Richard Callender's service and civilian bosses, visited and were impressed. Richard wrote to us: 'It was an extremely useful visit as they both found it most interesting and are completely sold on the idea that the Arboretum is the ideal location for the new Armed Forces Memorial. We now need to convince the Secretary of State for Defence.'

They did, and it was with great relief that on 18 March 2002 we listened to Geoff Hoon making the following announcement to the House of Commons about the location of the Armed Force Memorial: 'A project team was appointed early last year to look at potential sites...Extensive research was carried out [and] there has been wide consultation with the Services and ex-Service organisations on both the siting and criteria issues and there is general support for the proposals. I am delighted to be able to confirm that the Armed Forces Memorial will be sited at the National Memorial Arboretum in Staffordshire.'

In accordance with the inclusive philosophy that we had always held to at the NMA the Secretary of State also stated that the memorial would include those members of the Royal Fleet Auxiliary and Merchant Navy who were killed in conflict zones. It would be impossible to underestimate the importance of Geoff Hoon's decision and its positive impact on our future.

CHAPTER SIX

Lilac, Holly, Hazel, Rose and Rosemary: Women at War and Peace

Love is like the wild rose-briar;
Friendship like the holly-tree,
The holly is dark when the rose-briar blooms,
But which will bloom most constantly?

Emily Brontë

This chapter is dedicated to Jackie Fisher, whose hard work, joyous enthusiasm, leadership, commonsense, friendliness and determination made her a vital creative force at the National Memorial Arboretum.

I was once told by a lady in the Turkish countryside that one glance at the surrounding fields would prove that the word 'farmer' was not a masculine noun. The involvement of many uniformed women's organisations in the NMA proved also that 'soldier' was not a masculine word nor war solely a male activity. Although men may sow the seed it is often women and children who have to reap the bitter harvest and survive on it for many years. If the idea of remembrance brings to mind a long line of men marching past the Cenotaph on Remembrance Sunday, then we forget a most important element of remembrance – women. Those men march to pay tribute to lost comrades, but every war means women have to mourn and remember lost husbands, lovers, fiancés, brothers, fathers and sons. Every war produces its war widows who have often had to bring up children in much more strained circumstances than they ever would have imagined on the day that they married. Yet they have borne their grief and sorrow with great dignity and in many cases overcome adversity to raise children of whom their fathers would have been proud.

The opening appeal to create the Arboretum had, naturally, been linked to planting memorial trees and, of course, many war widows had made a contribution to have their husbands lives remembered in this way, but along, with a War Widows' Wood came the idea that the NMA should create a plot that would be a gift to this very special group rather than being created from monies that they might be asked to contribute. It was also considered appropriate that this plot should be planted in close proximity to the Chapel. This was for three reasons. The first was in response to those telling lines from the 27th verse in the first Chapter of the Letter of Saint James:

> Pure religion and undefiled before God and the Father is this, To visit the fatherless and widows in their affliction.

The second was to remind all our visitors that in any conflict, but especially those of the twentieth century and onwards, the majority of victims have been the innocent, the non-combatants, and that wars leave behind many wounds that never heal. The third was that a rose garden, which is what we intended to create, would be a wonderful welcome with which to greet visitors as they walked in.

The buildings of the Arboretum had been designed along the lines of a medieval monastery, for we wanted visitors to feel immediately upon entry that they were withdrawing from a world of bustle and business outside. Thus the long main building represented the main church entered at the West door, while to one side a cloistered way ran around to the Chapel which was where a chapter house might have been. In the square in between we placed both the rose garden and a plot designed as a tribute to those other innocent victims of war – young children.

As with so many of the project's schemes, the best way to pay tribute to the War Widows became obvious shortly after the need became apparent – a rose garden. But it needed to be a rose garden full of symbolism and designed in sympathy with the views and experience of the ladies themselves. It seemed logical, therefore, to turn to a lady designer for inspiration, and when Michael Marriott, the nursery manager of *David Austin Roses* at nearby Wolverhampton, proposed Dr Katherine Swift, a restorer of historic gardens and a designer steeped in tradition, she seemed a most appropriate choice.

Katherine immediately fell for the project and its potential. For inspiration she began with *The Flower* written by George Herbert, the seventeenth century priest and poet, especially its first two verses:

> How fresh, O Lord, how sweet and clean
> Are thy returns! Ev'n as the flowers in Spring;

To which, besides their own demean,
The late-past frosts tributes of pleasure bring;
Grief melts away
Like snow in May,
As if there were no such cold thing.

Who would have thought my shrivel'd heart
Could have recover'd greeness? It was gone
Quite underground; as flowers depart
To see their mother-root when they are blown;
Where they together
All hard weather,
Dead to the world, keep house unknown.

Katherine imagined that long hard journey that the grieving widows had to make through shock of bereavement and realisation of loss to eventual reconciliation and peace. It could never be an easy journey and each sad traveller would have had to make the most of it by themselves with many a period of despondency, despair, lack of progress or false turns. To symbolise the difficulty of that journey Katherine devised a unicursal (single-path) maze to express the idea of progress towards an ultimate spiritual goal. Along this path there were to be four gardens, each one representing a different stage of the journey as reflected in the colour of the flowers. Thus the roses selected started with the dark reds of love, sacrifice, spilt blood and death and moved through the purple of despair and neglect to a 'grey garden' showed the start of recovery and order but still retaining purples and mauves, the Victorian colours of 'half-mourning'. Beyond the 'grey garden' was a garden of memories and hope, with white and pink flowers of which the final rose was to be 'Peace' as a sign of hope for both the individual and the nation. Among the roses were to be planted narrow junipers and *Cupressus sempervirens*, symbols of both mourning and eternal life.

Katherine also wished the garden to be in flower for as much of the year as was possible. Her season would begin in May with the early yellow species roses such as *Rosa primula* (the incense rose) followed by *Rosa x Richardii* (the Holy Rose of Abyssinia). In June and July most of the old rose species would be in flower including the velvety-purple '*Cardinal de Richelieu*' and the white climber '*Mme. Alfred Carrière*', along with the purple and grey petalled '*Robert de Diable*' and the blush-pink moss rose, '*Comtesse de Murinais*'. As the season developed so the special attributes of David Austin's repeat-flowering English roses, including the beautifully scented '*Gertrude Jekyll*' and the gleaming white '*Winchester Cathedral*'. The planting of both '*Peace*' and '*The Pilgrim*' summed up the symbolism of the

Garden, where the roses, when design allowed, were chosen from those named after ladies.

Just ahead of Remembrance Sunday 1996, Baroness Strange, the ebullient President of the War Widow's Association, launched an Appeal to raise the £20,000 that was needed to plant the Rose Garden; and on the Saturday before Remembrance Sunday, the very supportive *The Daily Telegraph* printed a two page article about the Garden with several gloriously coloured illustrations by Beverley Fry – just part of the wonderfully creative work that she undertook for the Arboretum over many years.

Individual war widows told their own stories to add poignancy to the overall picture that we were trying to create. This showed how great a debt the nation owed to these ladies whose own natural inclination was to shun the limelight and live with their private grief. Just one can serve to sum up their dignity and faithfulness. A very elderly lady mentioned the fact that she had married on a Friday in 1917 and that her husband sailed away, never to return, on the Saturday. When asked whether she had considered marrying again she replied, "Yes, but it would not have been right!" Sadly, the conflicts in which Britain was to become involved after the Garden was planted meant that among our visitors there were many much younger war widows whose husbands had fallen in Northern Ireland, Afghanistan and Iraq. Another area of sadness was meeting several war-fiancées who had also remained true to their departed loved ones but felt that they had no support group or government pension which could provide them with solace or succour.

The very prominent position of the Rose Garden meant that we would be very late in planting it, for nothing could be started until all the building work was complete. This caused understandable friction, as did every delay in developing plots for Veterans linked to the Second World War, most of whom were reaching the age when they would soon require support to visit the site or would be too frail to venture out. We were in an obvious quandary: we could either rush things so that the Veterans could see, at the least, the start of their plot, or tell them to wait until everything was complete, by which time many of their number would have passed away. The same applied to the War Widows, for whom we had to plant a small, temporary rose garden which could be dedicated some years before we could create the final layout. Baroness Strange and her Committee were most understanding but they did urge us to push on as fast as possible. And with due reason; before the Garden was fully planted Lady Strange herself died, her contribution to the organisation being marked by a small sundial on the edge of the Garden.

Katherine's initial design had to be adjusted to fit the space available and to take onboard the practicalities of the site itself. Nevertheless, it makes a welcoming and reflective introduction to the whole site, just the qualities that we wished for. As visitors enter the Cloister and stand before the Rose Garden they can read a poem written by another lady, Estelle Lawrence, *Please Remember*:

> We leave for you a gift: this graceful garden,
> Its gentle sounds, sweet scents and glorious views,
> A place to walk, to meditate and muse,
> To pause and learn of those whose lives were broken.
>
> We hope that you will wander and peruse,
> Will contemplate a time passed out of reach,
> Will know as you survey these slender trees
> Grown tall and strong – small groves, grand avenues,
> Of oak and elm, of lime and ash and beech -
> What price was paid to save your liberties.
>
> We are the children and the grandchildren,
> The wives, the friends, of people still held dear;
> Whose sacrifice is celebrated here.
> Their lives touched ours: we will remember them.
> We wish that you who see these trees mature
> Shall cherish in your turn their memories.
> May all of those to whom we chose to pay
> Our tributes, futures lost or changed through war,
> Be honoured here by you for ever; please,
> Do not forget why they gave their today.

Beyond it, both appropriately and applicable to the whole site, we placed a plinth showing a map of the world covered with red dots. At the bottom of the map we drew two of the distinctive Commonwealth War Grave head-stones. One states, 'The Red Dots indicate the location by Country of the War Graves of Britain's fallen. The Seas cover their own dead'. The other, with a sprig of rosemary and a poppy growing beside it, states 'Dedicated to the courage of all War Widows'. That single word, 'Courage', is the motto of the War Widows' Association and it is singularly appropriate. It was thus a delight that Courage Brewers saw fit to make a generous dona-tion towards the Rose Garden. What was not a delight was to know that even as the garden was being planted more British ladies were qualifying for the most unwelcome status of War Widow.

The War Widows' Association was the first of many women's organisations to become involved with the Arboretum. The next one, 'Inner Wheel', whose membership was made up of the womenfolk of Rotarians, brought with it a remarkable lady whose involvement with the Arboretum was to be a significant and highly effective one.

When Jackie Fisher knew that she was to be the Chairman of Number Six District, Inner Wheel, having been President of her local Lichfield St Chad's Branch, she started thinking about which Charity she would choose to support during her time in office. She was looking for something that would be not only local but one where her members' contribution could be seen to make a difference. While thinking about this she came across an article about the proposed Arboretum and got in touch. I went to see her.

My first and lasting impression was of a lady who had a determination to do the best with whatever she set her hand to and the capability of making things happen. Also, as highly active and respected local citizens, Jackie and her husband David knew and were listened to by key players in both business and local government. If they had done little else but arrange introductory meetings they would have made a massive contribution to the cause; but they did a lot more.

I was introduced to the ladies of Inner Wheel at their district conference, at which Jackie had introduced the idea of the Arboretum with such enthusiasm that the project there and then, gained its first very local supporters. From here Jackie took the project to national level, ending with me addressing the Inner Wheel national conference at Bournemouth – a room of four thousand people of whom I was the only one not wearing a hat!

Inner Wheel agreed not only to raise money for the project but to establish a plot dedicated to their various branches. In a way this was a departure from the original aim of the site as a tribute to the wartime generations of the twentieth- century but many of these ladies were giving in tribute to fathers or brothers lost in action, while the organisation itself, dedicated to serving the community, pointed the way to the site becoming one where the work of all such groups of 'givers' could be acknowledged.

For the Inner Wheel plot we took their badge of a cogged golden wheel and recreated it with plants. A circle of golden-leaved elms, *Ulmus x hollandica*, 'Dampieri Aurea', a narrow conical tree which is unaffected by Dutch elm disease was planted, and beneath it rosemary, both for its blue flowers and its symbolism of remembrance. Having raised the funds for the plot, Jackie was hooked on the idea of the Arboretum and wished to help further. She thus undertook to act as the volunteer local contact and from that became the programme and event organiser, continuing in an unpaid role until funds were available for her to become the full-time site manager. In this position she established the Arboretum's reputation both as a welcoming institutiom and one which was determined to have a go at most things with a 'can do' attitude. In those early years it was important that, whatever arose, we were able to handle it with our small staff which consisted mostly of volunteer ladies. Everyone had to turn their hand to whatever was required to make the show run smoothly. Thus we all became adept at cleaning, laying up, waiting at and clearing tables, hosing down, and serving in the shop, along with directing and parking traffic and speaking about the project to every one who came, from junior school children to VIPs. This was over and above helping plant and label trees, cut grass, weed plots and skirmish for litter. We never had anyone refuse to do even the least pleasant of tasks.

The second plot in the cloisters, which completed the verse from St James's Epistle quoted earlier, was 'The Garden of the Innocents', which was very much the inspiration of Jackie Fisher and the ladies of the Inner Wheel. They felt that we should acknowledge the hurt done to young children in times of war by adults who, twenty centuries after the teaching of the 'Prince of Peace', should have found better ways to deal with international disagreements. Jackie also felt strongly that the plants in the garden should be just green and white in colour: green for youth and white for innocence.

Before the site could be prepared we had our first tree to be placed there. On 11 November 1999 at our Remembrance Day Service we dedicated an Elder, *Sambucus nigra*, in tribute to Anne Frank and those of her generation who, like her, were victims of Nazi concentration camps. An elder was chosen because Anne Frank died after someone betrayed her hiding place. Ancient British legend recounts that Judas Iscariot hung himself on an elder tree in remorse having betrayed Jesus (it must have been a particularly fine specimen). At the end of one Millennium and the start of another it seemed appropriate to link these two acts separated by almost two thousand years. The white elder flowers would symbolise the innocence of youth, but we arranged with the local Inner Wheel Club that every 12 June, Anne Frank's birthday, their members would come to the Arboretum and pick the flowers so that the tree will never fruit, making it a symbol of all those lives that have been denied the chance to reach maturity.

While Anne Frank's tree was being planted, these words were read out by Michael Rosen of the Anne Frank Educational Trust:

> We hope that anyone who knows of this tree
> Will remember Anne Frank.
> We hope that anyone who knows of this tree
> Will remember how from her attic window
> Anne Frank watched a tree growing outside
> And was so moved and entranced
> She couldn't speak.
> We hope that anyone who knows of this tree
> Will remember how Anne Frank lost her life.

We hope that anyone who knows of this tree
Will never let such things happen again.
We hope that anyone who knows of this tree
Will have as much hope in their hearts and minds as Anne Frank did.

The Garden of the Innocents was designed around a number of raised beds shaped like pieces of a jigsaw: a puzzle that children play with and yet one which indicates the puzzlement that they feel when they suffer pain, grief, loss and injury through foul deeds being perpetrated around their homes by men at war.

April 2003 was a cruel month and, like the photograph from an earlier war of the young frightened Vietnamese girl running towards the camera, her arms scorched by napalm, one image from the Iraq war that was raging at that time seared itself on everyone's mind. It was the picture of twelve year old Ali Ismail Abbas who, going to sleep in the village of Zafaramiya, came out of unconsciousness to find one of his hands a twisted, blackened claw and his other arm burnt off at the elbow. The rest of his body was covered in third-degree burns. When he cried out for help no help came; his father, pregnant mother and brother, along with several other relatives had all died in the American missile strike that tore his home apart. The West had to wait for pictures of this cruelly orphaned boy until he had been cleaned up and was sitting up in bed in the al-Kindi hospital with his bandaged stumps. Nevertheless the image so seared the heart of the public that the Hospital Director was forced to address the press scrambling for more pictures: 'Why do you all want to talk to Ali? There are hundred of children suffering like him.'

Back in England I took the picture of Ali into my office and placed it beside my sketches for the 'Garden of the Innocents'. The resemblance that the mutilated child had to one of my jigsaw pieces made me tremble. At that moment Ali's sorrow and the reason for it became a part of 'The Garden of the Innocents'. If we wanted any reason to explain why we were creating it, this poor child had provided it.

When the time came for planting the plot the Tamworth branch of B&Q donated most of the bedding plants and shrubs; they grew well and the pure white flowers soon made the plot an eye-catching one and a strong contrast to the deep reds and purples across the path in the War Widows' Rose Garden.

While the Inner Wheel site moved the Arboretum's focus away from exclusively paying tribute to those who served with military or uniformed civilian organisations, the plot next to the Inner Wheel broke totally new ground and, like so many of the projects, it came about through an entirely unrelated initiative. In my search for kindred but more experienced and professional sylvanophiles, I had called on the Tree Council to elicit their support which, as with every tree organisation, had been given willingly. Among the small team that formed the professional staff of the Tree Council was Jon Stokes, who had organised for the Arboretum to plant a grove of trees to celebrate the creation of the hundredth tree warden scheme. Jon was also a member of SANDS, the Still Born and Neo Natal Death Society, who were seeking an appropriate spot where they could plant a memorial to their lost children. The idea of having the memorial at the Arboretum was never a problem to me; what I needed to do was see how it could be made to fit in logically. The dreadful reality of war formed the link. Whatever romantic idea of war lingers in anyone's imagination there is no such thing as a 'clean' conflict. Civilian deaths have always featured and, horrifically, in the wars of the twentieth century civilian casualties overtook military ones with the introduction of bombing and the growth of civil war and terrorism. Women, away from the front, suffer not only through the loss of their menfolk but through disease, deprivation, destruction, rape and miscarriage; they are witness to the loss of at least two generations of their families, one of whom will never be born or survive infancy. We could get across this message of the disaster that war is for ordinary homes through the SANDS Plot. Their suggestion was approved and the Arboretum gained its first plot planted with mature trees and designed by a professional. As such it served as a demonstration of what the rest of the site could look like in a few years' time. It also included two massive wooden seats carved out of single trunks of elm whose sinuous shape imitated the twist of the Garden Path and provided a place where the visitor could reflect on the plot and their own emotions. And it was an emotional plot. Lying beside a central 'teardrop' was a small stone table on which lay a sensitively carved figure of a stillborn child. There was nothing mawkish about the sculpture and it was touching to see, on the day the Plot was dedicated, how the young children so gently brushed their hands over the figure in a caress.

The third women's group from a non-military background to ask to become involved in the Arboretum were the Trefoil Guild, ladies who had been Girl Guides in their youth and retained an interest in that movement. For them I proposed a plot using pleached limes to form a large trefoil shape. It was neither an original nor an eye-catching idea and in the end it failed, but not before I had spent several years ignoring the fact that the trees did not like their location which lay directly below the east side of the mound on which the Visitor Centre had been constructed. Once planted, the limes flourished for a few months but looked very dead by the Spring, while their replacements were very dead the following Spring. Searching for a reason and an excuse to make to the sponsoring ladies, I found that for some reason water draining from the car park collected just below ground level at the Trefoil site – the roots of the trees were being waterlogged.

Although we had drainage put in it was always going to be a soggy area, but it was also the only area that we had available for the Trefoil Guild. The solution came during a visit to the National Botanic Garden of Wales where a similar damp area was verdant with willow-weave sculptures. Returning, fired up with this idea, I found that our wildlife enthusiast, Richard Thorpe, had a friend who was an expert willow weaver. The new Trefoil now had an exciting area of woven huts and tunnels and became well used by our younger visitors, which was precisely what the Guild ladies had wanted it to be; success but only just.

Another ladies' group whose views were in accord with those of the Arboretum were the Soroptimists, whose plot was placed within the United Nations Circle close to the International Friendship Garden. This was a fun plot to design as we were able to replicate their badge, which shows the rays of a rising sun, by using golden laurel radiating from gravel paths, all of which was surrounded by a laurel hedge.

Yet, although civilian women's organisations were to play a prominent part in the creation of the Arboretum, the main groups involved were, naturally, the Services such as the WRNS, WRAC and WAAFA, together with the medical arms of the QARANC and QARNNS. It would certainly be true to say that they were generally more determined to have their plot and to be involved in its creation than most of their male colleagues. Indeed, they played a role out of all proportion to their relative strength as units in the armed forces.

The WRNS joined up with the Queen Alexandra's Royal Naval Nursing Sisters to have a combined plot alongside the Naval Review. This was to take the form of a large square enclosed by beech, inside of which a path in the shape of an anchor led to two memorial gardens. One of these, planted with the pale blues of lavender and rosemary reflected the colour of the WRNS badges, while the other, with red and gold, mostly buddleia and euonymus, showed the colours of the Sisters' uniform. At the anchor ring end a small bower was dedicated to the Voluntary Aid Detachment (VAD) RN. The Association of WRNS had also asked that the planting provide shelter for small birds, especially wrens, and encourage butterflies, hence the buddleia. These were very positive suggestions for a site that was bleak and windswept, and the sighting of the first red admiral on a buddleia was a joy to us all. In addition, we had left space for a few trees that would give both blossom and fruit for the insects and birds as well as raise the visitors' eyes above the level of the shrubs.

The Association of WRNS had planned to dedicate their plot on 5 June 1999, presuming that the weather should be fine at that time of year. It was not, but a large marquee protected everyone from the cold during the Service which was conducted by the Chaplain of the Fleet, the Venerable Simon Golding. In many ways the involvement of the Association of

WRNS symbolised all that was good about the concept of the Arboretum. When their Chairman, Eleanor Patrick, first visited the site she had to walk across a grassless, muddy, featureless field to see a plot that was pegged out in no great detail; in fact it was worse than it should have been because rabbits had managed to eat all the initial beech hedging. Luckily, Eleanor saw immediately the potential and the need for her members to be involved. It was that vision and determination by her and all the other groups who came along at the beginning that ensured that the Arboretum would be a success however small its beginnings. Eleanor and several of her colleagues also got down on their hands and knees to help plant hedge and shrubs; from her photograph on the cover of the Association's magazine it is obvious that she enjoyed the work.

The Women's Royal Army Corps became involved through the Adjutant General's Corps, with which they had amalgamated and in whose plot they were to be represented. However, they decided that the Corps needed its own plot, and we were able to offer them one at the end of Giffard Avenue. The square in which they were to be established cried out for a bold shape and it was felt that a large W-shaped bed would be an appropriate design. It was also agreed that it should be a colourful plot, so we planted a collection of lilacs all of which carried girls' names. These ranged from the pure white panicles of *Syringa* 'Maud Notcutt' through the pale pink spring flowers of *Syringa x hyacinthiflora* 'Esther Staley' and the deeper pink of *prestoniae* 'Audrey' to the dark purplish red of *prestoniae* 'Elinor', with many other colours in between. At the back of the plot Hazel and Holly 'Golden King', a masculine name but a female tree, made reference both to the Corps Regimental March, 'The Nut Brown Maiden', and the fact that they were so often called upon to do tasks that had previously been assumed could only be done by men.

How best to create a site for the Women's Auxiliary Air Force was as perplexing as it had been to design one to fit the awkward shape of the RAF plot in whose boundaries it needed to fit. Once again the answer came, appropriately enough, from the heavens. Standing outside one evening watching that marvellous comet, Hale-Bopp, disappear in to the darkening western sky, I stayed on to watch the stars come out, when my eyes focussed on the W-shaped constellation Cassiopeia, named after an Ethiopian Queen who was placed in the heavens. All the ingredients were there, including the right number of trees. So was sketched the WAAF Association plot in which it was intended to plant trees with a link to the stars, such as *Magnolia* 'Galaxy', *Magnolia stellata* and *Prunus subhirtella* 'Stellata'. Unfortunately, the exposed nature of the site at the start would mean a delay in planting these delightful specimens, but once they had become established the WAAFA plot would a most popular spot for visitors.

The women's military associations brought with them the very human story of romance in uniform, sometime whirlwind, sometimes happy, sometimes sad, often too hot not to cool down. Corporal Sylvia Pickering kept a record of her meeting and subsequent days out with a young Australian aircrewman, Sergeant Tom Whitely, a navigator with 467/463 Australian Lancaster Squadron. Their cycle rides in the Lincolnshire countryside around RAF Waddington tell a joyfully innocent tale of two young people becoming truly fond of each other. Then, on 6 October 1944, Tom's Lancaster took off for a raid over Germany and disappeared without trace. The crew were presumed dead. Sylvia tried to rebuild her shattered life. At the end of April 1945 her telephone rang and it was Tom, just released from captivity in Germany. His plane had crashed and he and the two surviving members of the crew had been taken as prisoners of war. Sylvia was delighted but had to tell Tom of her recent engagement. After a few minutes Tom rang off and, although Sylvia's engagement was later broken off, they never met or corresponded again. In the enormity of war's great griefs the failure of these two to marry the one they truly loved is a small footnote. However, footnotes often explain far more clearly what we fail to understand in the text.

The plots for each of the women's branches of the armed services were not the only ones dedicated to ladies in uniform. Once it had been announced that the Royal Artillery were to have their own plot a formidable little lady from Nuneaton, Vee Robinson, contacted the Arboretum to say that she would raise the money to purchase the adjacent plot for the ATS RA, a group that encompassed a great number of women who had manned searchlights during the Second World War. Vee was a lady who one knew was going to achieve what she set out to do. When she said she would raise £5,000 through 'demanding' £5 from one thousand ex-ATS ladies one felt that none of them would have the temerity to refuse. They didn't. Vee's plot was secured. It was planted at her request as an orchard, with one exception. In one corner we placed a golden *leylandi*, 'Robinson's Gold', in tribute to Vee.

One of the continuing delights for those involved with the creation of the Arboretum was that we all learnt something new most days. Thus war time groups we had never heard of got in touch to tell us their story. One such was the Women's Auxiliary Service Burma or WAS(B), known as the Chinthe Women because of the image of the mythological creature that formed their badge. The WAS(B) were a 250 strong team of ladies who managed mobile and static canteens throughout the Burma campaign. Indeed, their work might have been forgotten had not a mother and daughter, Sally and Lucy Jaffé not decided to find out what Lucy's grandmother, Ninian Taylor, who had been appointed OBE for her work, had done in the war. When Burma was overrun by the Japanese in 1942 a number of ladies who were working as encoders in the WAS(B) decided not to take the easier option of evacuation to England but remained behind to organise mobile canteens for front line troops. They performed this service not only in Burma but in Indonesia and eventually Japan itself, and were only disbanded in 1946 well after most of the troops had already gone home. During these years they shared the harsh conditions of the troops, constantly on the move, living under canvas and working 16 hour days. Often exhausted, soaked, sunburnt, tired and scared themselves, their cheerful presence was reckoned to be a major morale boost for an Army fighting against enormous odds and in appalling conditions. Indeed, Lieutenant General Sir Oliver Leese referred to the WAS(B) as 'the biggest single factor affecting the morale of forward troops'. An indication of their own dedication and morale can be gauged by the simple fact that, after the war ended, the girls used to argue with each other as to who would have the privilege of getting up at 0430 to greet and tend arriving prisoners of war who were being flown out of their camps. The memories that the Jaffés gathered all demonstrate that crucial skill of cheerfulness in adversity and ability to laugh in every fell circumstance. Now, knowing that both the Burma Star Association and the Far East POWs were having plots planted at the Arboretum, the Chinthe Women decided that they too should have their contribution remembered at the site.

The WAS(B) had started the war in Burma as encoders. Back in Britain there was another group, mainly females, who were also involved in signals: the 'Y' Group who intercepted enemy messages at Beaumanor for analysis at Bletchley Park. For years, standing by the clear instructions of the Official Secrets Act, they had kept their activities under wraps so that even some of their closest relatives never knew precisely what their contribution had been. The Arboretum provided them some fifty-five years later not only with a spot to pay tribute to their number but also an opportunity to tell their story.

The 'Y' Group were another of the site's early participants who wished their dedication to take place before their spot was ready for them. For them we had to plant into the reddish mud below the Visitor Centre mound with the understanding that the plants, a large 'Y'-shaped hedged Avenue with a memorial plinth in the centre and benches at the end, would be moved when it was appropriate to do so. The result was that, over the next few years, while we were preparing the site, we were being chivvied along by ladies impatient to see their plot established. When it was we were lucky that the successors to the 'Y' Group, Defence Special Signals School at Chicksands, were delighted to volunteer to make periodic visits to keep the plot tidy. In those early days while previously dormant dock and other weeds felt it worth endeavouring to become re-established such volunteer groups were a godsend. When one looked around the Arboretum at all the volunteers working there, one fully understood that 'gardener' just like 'farmer' was not a masculine noun.

CHAPTER SEVEN

Chestnuts and Truncheons: The Police and Emergency Services

Give me a land of boughs in leaf,
A land of trees that stand;
Where trees are fallen, there is grief;
I love no leafless land.

A. E. Housman

I f the Arboretum was to succeed as a national project it needed to demonstrate that it had local support. To this end I began wandering in to the Banks and Building Societies in Lichfield to ask their managers if they would help fund our activities, although they were, as yet, literally not off the ground. As so often in Lichfield there was every encouragement, and my confidence grew with every visit made, but it was a friend of the Fishers, John Haggett, a local solicitor who was to provide a massive breakthrough. John was a keen hockey player and through the sport had become great friends with the head of Police Mutual Assurance, Peter Sharpe, whose offices were in Lichfield. John arranged for me to call on Peter, whose organisation I knew nothing about and which was not on my list of potential supporters. Peter, an enthusiastic, charming and successful Chief Executive was much respected by the Police Service which he served and for whom he had achieved great things in his time at Police Mutual.

Rather naively, my first call on Peter was simply to discuss whether or not Police Mutual might be in a position to help fund the Arboretum. However, as our conversation developed it was obvious that Peter had in mind a much more active role for his organisation, which was to have a tribute to the Police Service created at the site. At this early stage with few areas in the design allocated to any group, it was soon a matter of discussing how best to achieve this aim.

What was very obvious from the start was that the police were very proud of their individual forces and that any national tribute would gain most support if each of these independent entities was recognised. The best way to achieve this was to plant a tree dedicated to each of the forces that covered the United Kingdom, and the thin blue line that this conjured up would be most suitable along an Avenue, redolent of the police lining a road. To achieve this with a gap of three metres between trees would require an Avenue some hundred metres long and we had just such an Avenue on our plan leading down from the Visitor Centre towards the Chetwynd Bridge over the River Tame which marked the boundary of the Arboretum. However, the first part of this Avenue was 300 metres long so we were going to need other Police organisations to become involved, and Peter was an ideal conduit to encourage their involvement.

Once the idea was agreed, Peter set up a working group formed from representatives of each of the representative groups within the police. Such a group was already in existence and met regularly at Police Mutual to monitor and discuss the work of the Company. They agreed to take on this extra task while Peter circulated a letter to each force inviting them to sponsor a tree for their own force with a sum that would also help cover the cost of preparing the Avenue itself. As our meetings were always followed by an excellent lunch, members of the working group never seemed to have to leave early; it worked well. One of the most enthusiastic of those members was Deputy Chief Constable David Rowley, who was approaching the end of his career and retired while the project was still maturing. A few days after his retirement David died suddenly and unexpectedly aged 58, having spent 42 years in the police service in which his wife Margaret's father and grandfather had also served. It was a very emotional experience planting beech trees in tribute to the three officers and siting a bench beside the Police Avenue, dedicated to David whom Margaret remembered as saying often during sylvan walks, 'I'm going to come back as a beech tree.' He has, and the weeping purple beech dedicated to his life is growing into one of the more beautiful trees on the site.

Early in our discussions the question as to what to call this Avenue was raised. In the boardroom at Police Mutual Assurance where we were meeting were copies of various in-house magazines and newsletters. One of these was called 'The Beat' and it seemed to me that this would be a most appropriate title; the suggestion was adopted in less than a minute and one of the most significant and effective pieces of planting within the Arboretum had a name.

For 'The Beat' had an importance beyond the police forces which it acknowledged. The Arboretum had been established initially to pay tribute to the men and women of the armed services. Very soon after the idea was born the Merchant Navy came on board, but even then it was their contribution to the war effort was what we were acknowledging. With the Police we began looking beyond the armed and merchant service to other uniformed organisations who make a major contribution to our nation's well being in peace as well as in war. At the beginning the idea was based upon the role of the Police in time of conflict, acknowledging those in the force who had died carrying out their duty in wartime; but there really was no logic in separating this group from others who had died on duty whatever the circumstances, nor in failing to recognise the valuable contribution made by all constabularies and their officers. After all it was often a case in the Police as in the armed forces that life or death could be a case of 'there but for fortune': a car crash with a miraculous escape; a bullet that missed a vital artery; the presence of first aid. And, of course, balancing lucky escapes were unlucky accidents. Survival by itself was no reason to differentiate between colleagues. We had not done so with the armed forces and there seemed to be no reason so to do with the Police.

The next question with which we were faced was to decide what type of tree would be appropriate. Once again a little bit of research and a lucky coincidence helped us to the logical answer. Just outside Lichfield lay the pleasure park, Drayton Manor, which had been the home of Sir Robert Peel, the founder of the police force. Jackie Fisher, in her role as President of the local District Inner Wheel, had arranged to hold her October AGM here, and when I had gone along to speak I arrived early and found scattered around the car park hundreds of conkers from venerable chestnuts which would have stood here at the time Robert Peel was in residence. I gathered several pockets full which I planted up. Then I discovered that the first truncheons were made from chestnut, a dense wood that would have given a miscreant a knock to remember. Given these two facts, there seemed to be no other more appropriate tree for 'The Beat' than the Horse Chestnut, *Aesculus hippocastanum*.

The planting of 'The Beat' brought into focus one of the presentational problems of the Arboretum which was how to concentrate interest on a flat site over which one could cast one's eye wherever one might be standing. Thus, on walking down 'The Beat' it was possible to see not only the plots on either side but also those several hundred metres ahead; the openness removed the thrill of discovery, making the site like an open plan office rather than a collection of rooms as in a stately home.

A rather grand stately home provided the answer. On a visit to Vienna, my wife Jane and I had walked through the grounds of several Hapsburg palaces which used chestnut to line their avenues. What they had done to add the interest of discovery of what lay beyond was to intersperse the planting with hedging of various types of which the most appropriate for the Arboretum seemed to be field maple, *Acer campestre*, which has a lovely leaf and fine autumn colours. The chestnuts along these Avenues were also rigorously clipped to keep their branches from spreading over the Avenue and creating gloom. The formal result seemed again appropriate for the group for whom they were being planted.

The need to ensure that 'The Beat' acknowledged all police officers was brought home both by the death of David Rowley and by a very early request to plant a memorial tree to PC Robert Dallow who had died in a car crash on 17 December 1995 whilst on duty. Robert was to have one of the trees grown from a Drayton Manor conker planted for him outside the quiet garden, where the benches for David Rowley were placed. Near to this another chestnut was planted to commemorate a Staffordshire policeman, James Adams, who, joining in 1951 at the age of 17 was, on his retirement in 2003, Britain's longest serving police officer.

'The Beat' had been planned so that anyone standing in the Long Gallery of the Visitor Centre could look straight down it. At one of our meetings a police officer suggested that a large wooden statue of a policeman, then languishing in a gym at their staff college at Bramshill in Hampshire, might welcome being returned to the public gaze at the Arboretum, where he could be placed in the Gallery almost as a way of introducing 'The Beat'. A visit to Bramshill convinced me that this seven foot giant, carved from the trunk of an elm, would indeed welcome returning to public duties and we arranged for him to be brought to the site. A plan for a welcoming event was put into place but, unfortunately, the Visitor Centre was falling behind schedule and it was necessary for the welcoming group to walk along duckboards and large carpets of industrial polythene to welcome our ever alert policeman. Good humour and understanding saved the day.

Good humour was also very evident when 'The Beat' was officially opened by the Home Secretary, Jack Straw, on 8 September 1997. Peter Sharpe had ensured that every police force in the country sent a senior representative and that all the guests were provided with an umbrella and galoshes, for 'The Beat' itself, apart from the trees, was a long expanse of brown earth. Jack Straw, who planted the tree for the Metropolitan Police, the only force over which he exercised direct control, managed to talk to everyone. The Labour Party had only just come to power and the Home Secretary was very new in post, in charge of a most important, high-profile and complicated Department of State. He must have had both very full in-trays and pressing matters to resolve. One would not have guessed that. He spent most of the day with Peter Sharpe and the Constabulary representatives and seemed neither to be in a hurry to move nor to show anything but a hundred per cent interest in every conversation. He spoke several times without reference to his notes and was full of questions. A bravura performance. Some years later the Arboretum was visited by a

Minister of State who had come to plant a tree for the Tree Council. She read each word from a prepared speech which she seemed not to have seen before she got up to speak; she wore city shoes, asked no questions and moved on rapidly to her next engagement. A most noticeable contrast.

After Jack Straw had completed the official planting, each force representative found their particular tree and was photographed beside it and the bright blue plaque on which their constabulary crest was displayed. Then nearly every one of them insisted on having a photograph taken by the Royal Ulster Constabulary tree along with the Deputy Chief Constable who had flown over for the occasion. That was one of those vignettes which showed the great respect in which that gallant force was held and a clear indication of how much it deserved the award of the George Cross a few years later when it was reformed as the Police Service of Northern Ireland.

The RUC also answered for us the question of what we should do with the unallocated trees between the ones dedicated to constabularies. There were several other Northern Ireland constabulary units which were no longer extant and the RUC asked for them to be remembered on our site as well. As the RUC tree had been planted in front of the plot dedicated to the Royal Irish Regiment this gave the Arboretum its first 'Irish' area. Later many who had served in forces that no longer existed, through amalgamations, also requested a tree so in a very short space of time every tree, along 'The Beat' had a dedicatory plaque.

News of 'The Beat' spread to other civilian services and it was not long before the Fire Service was asking whether they might also be represented. The Fire Service approach provided an interesting contrast to that of the Police. Both were established as individual forces, but whereas the Police wanted their memorial to reflect their individuality as constabularies, the Fire Service wanted a plot that would show them as a united organisation. The plot we selected lay alongside another major path, Giffard Avenue, named after Peter Giffard, a major philanthropist and local President of the Country Landowners Association whose son, John, was the Chief Constable of Staffordshire. As with 'The Beat' the drive to create the Fire & Rescue Service Plot came from one man. Jeff Ord was the Chief Fire Officer of Northumberland when, in April 1996, he read in *The Daily Telegraph* about the proposal to plant the Northern Ireland plot at the NMA and felt that the contribution by the 'heroic group of men and women' of the British Fire Service should be similarly recognised at the site. I was delighted as I had failed to interest wartime Veterans of the Fire Service in the scheme. With a senior Fire Chief involved, and Jeff Ord was moving on and up, firstly to South Yorkshire and then Strathclyde, our chances of getting the Firemen onboard was greatly improved. And so it proved to be, with Jeff's team at Sheffield, principally his enthusiastic Divisional

Officers, Keith Gill and Andy Heald, doing all the hard work that resulted in every Brigade joining in.

The design for the Fire Service plot was based around a drill tower, one of those tall square steel framed structures which dominate Fire Stations and are so immediately recognisable, around which would be planted shrubs linked to smoke, flame and fire. The tower itself would have fire thorn, *Pyracantha*, climbing up it, while the path approaching it would be lined with varieties of Smoke tree (*Cotinus*), and *Senecio* to simulate smoke and flame. The problem was finding a redundant drill tower. After several years one became available in nearby Market Bosworth and the Fire Service arranged for it to be brought over to the Arboretum where it languished for many month lying horizontally until the funding became available to raise it up. Sadly, after a few years on site it was decided that for Health and Safety reasons it would have to come down; one of my very earliest ideas for the Arboretum had a very short life indeed.

The close links with the Fire Service led to the creation of another memorial plinth that paid tribute to the British victims of the collapse of the Twin Towers in New York. The New York Fire Service had been supported after 9/11 by a contingent of Fire & Rescue personnel from the United Kingdom headed by Chief Fire Officer David O'Dwyer of Hereford & Worcester Fire & Rescue Service. On completion the team were presented with some of the debris from 'ground zero'. This they passed on to the NMA to be inserted in a plinth beside the small tribute plot that we had planted, which consisted of two giant Redwoods to represent the Twin Towers, a Scots Pine, a Welsh Yew, an Irish Strawberry Tree, an English Oak and an American Black oak, all donated by the Arboricultural Association.

Next to the Fire Service plot we allocated one for Civil Defence, thus linking two groups with a close and vital working relationship in times of crisis. Tim Essex-Lopresti and Patrick Stanton of the Civil Defence Association wanted to place two large monoliths at the site. Using one of these as the focal point it was possible to imitate the organisation's badge of a triangle surrounded by a circle of stars by planting a ring of *Malus* 'Red Sentinel' around the stone, providing a link to the duties of Civil Defence during the Cold War. The larger stone paid tribute to the almost 2 million volunteers who served with Civil Defence in World War Two, especially remembering the 7,000 who died. The smaller stone then became a tribute to all the working animals lost in conflict.

The Ambulance Service took a lot longer to come on board but in so doing were able to have a plot right alongside the entrance to the Arboretum and adjacent to the one dedicated to all who had served with Queen Alexandra's Royal Nursing Corps.

Centred in the Heart of England, the Arboretum is some 65 miles from the nearest salt water and one of the furthest inland places in the British

Isles. It came as a surprise, therefore, to discover that nearby Tamworth was home to one of the most active branches of the Royal National Lifeboat Institute (RNLI). This was due to the very keen coterie gathered around their Chairman, Miss Chris Muspratt. Chris had witnessed the various tributes being erected to voluntary agencies at the Arboretum and felt that the RNLI should be among those represented. Her main difficulty was to convince other branches that the NMA was both a suitable place for such a memorial and that the project would justify the effort needed to raise funds apart from those restricted to supporting the ongoing work of the RNLI. There was also the question of to whom this memorial was to be dedicated. Indeed, for me a major question was whether we were talking about a memorial or a tribute. Memorials tend to be dedicated to those who have lost their lives in the course of duty and those for the volunteer crews of the lifeboats are among the most poignant. Yet the heroic work of the coxswains and crews of the lifeboat would not be possible without the hard work and dedication of those who run the shore side operation and the volunteers who raise the money to pay for their boats and equipment. These modest people found it difficult to believe that their devotion should be recognised alongside that of their gallant crews, but this was in fact one of the aims of the project.

While Chris and her team were beavering away at fund raising we had the much easier and more enjoyable task of designing the RNLI plot. With the River Tame as one of our boundaries we were able to select a spot past which water flowed down to the sea, thus linking their garden to the waters in which they did their rescue work. And as with the Fire Service there was one iconic structure with which everyone associated the RNLI – the boat houses from which the lifeboat were launched, models of which were once used as their collecting tins. But how to recreate a Boat House?

The failure to establish lime trees in the Trefoil Guild Plot had led to our introducing willow-weave structures on that damp site. The willow weave artist was more than willing to discuss how best to make a boat house in this manner and we were thus able to plant one with a slipway leading down to the Tame. At the end of the slipway we created, courtesy of Lafarge Aggregates, nearby works, a sandy beach upon whose surface Friends were to scatter shells and seaweed brought back every time they went on a visit to the seaside. A small willow-weave boat completed the beach, while overlooking it another fine piece of sculpture was created on site from a massive piece of stone by Andrew Fitchett, a local craftsman. When completed the site looked superb and it rapidly became one of the favourites with the visiting public.

A postman delivering the mail whether by bike or on foot or in van is one of those quintessential British sights that produce an immediate feeling of well-being – a 'God's in his heaven, all's well with the world' sort of moment. Associating this peaceful activity with the violence of war is not easy but through two world wars the General Post Office, as it then was, did a vital and often dangerous task. Many postmen joined up and in the First World War the Post Office Rifles won forty Military Crosses and 160 Military Medals, while Sergeant Alfred J Knight was awarded the Victoria Cross. As in so many similar units the cost was high: 1,800 Riflemen were killed and some 4,000 more wounded during the fighting. In the Second World War many Post Office workers transferred to the Royal Corps of Signals and it was one of these, Denis Roberts, who returned to the GPO and rose to be a senior manager, who came up with the idea that the service of the GPO should be remembered at the Arboretum.

Denis had first come across the NMA through his First Army connections for he had served in the 5th (London) Corps Signals who had planted a tree in the Mediterranean Plot. Although the GPO no longer existed Denis had connection in both its successor entities, British Telecom and the Post Office, both of whom made generous donations to create the brick-built plinth which was to serve as a tribute to GPO personnel and present an account of their exploits. For the design we chose a few rows of black bricks surmounted by several rows of red taking it up to the height of a pillar box. A 'garden path' led up to the plinth while the use of green, the old GPO colour, and red continued in the choice of plants within the plot. One of these was *Liquidambar* 'Lane Roberts', another example of the way in which we tried to link the instigators of plots with the plots themselves.

CHAPTER EIGHT

The Tribute of the Trees: Individual Memorials

Then spoke the tree, and all the forest near
Took up the words with deepening strength and power –
'Spring is the symbol of the soul's re-birth,
The resurrection of a life more fair,
More beautiful than any earth can give.
Whatever storms and tempests may have been,
Whatever sorrows drenched the world with tears,
Spring must return, the note of hope will sound,
Something rekindles in the frozen heart,
And in the doubting spirit something stirs –
The warmth, the comfort of returning faith,
The certainty of greater life beyond.'

Marjorie Crosbie

It was obvious from very early on that the Arboretum project was principally not about trees but about people. This might seem strange for a concept involving the planting of thousands of trees but not when one realized that most of those trees by themselves represented the wishes and told the stories of hundreds of people. Even a memorial so individual as 'Shot at Dawn' not only brings to mind the fate of 350 young men, it also recalls the impact that fate had on their families and friends, those who passed sentence and those who carried it out. Every tree planted in the Ulster Ash Grove not only recalls the person whose name appears on it but also pays tribute to those who knew them, who loved and miss them. Stories of terror, of heroism and loss are there to be plucked and tasted like fruit from each tree planted in the Merchant Navy Convoy or the pair of cypresses that stand as green scrolls ready to tell of noble deeds wrought by the Rats of Tobruk. Everywhere it is the same. The Arboretum is a living library whose tree trunks are but covers concealing thousands of stories. They have within their bark almost the whole record of the activities of British citizens, service and civilian, through a violent century of war, conflict and confrontation. Walk around the site as if passing through serried shelves of archives, select a dedicated tree at random, and its story can hold your interest for a lifetime. So, although people walking around the Arboretum will see the trees, their attention is drawn to the purpose of the plot and the individuals recalled by it. Indeed, the project began with writing to the hundreds of people who had supported Leonard Cheshire's War Memorial Fund for Disaster Relief with a donation in memory of an individual and asking them if they were prepared to sponsor a tree in tribute to the same person. It was the willingness of this particular group to do so that not only convinced us there was a need to establish the Arboretum but also provided the initial funding to support our early months of work.

Someone once worked out that if the numbers of those involved in the creation of the Arboretum either directly, indirectly or through inference were added up it would mean that the project was by far the most popular of all the Millennium schemes, far outweighing, thank goodness, the Dome, and even, in the number of its donors, having more support than the wonderful and highly successful Eden Project in Cornwall.

It was very obvious to us that we were writing to an elderly generation, many of whom could afford very little to have a tree planted. For this reason we 'suggested' a donation of £30 but made it clear that no one would be turned away if they gave less. In this we were gambling that a few more generous gifts might compensate for the smaller ones, and they did – just! But the gifts from those early donors were worth a great deal more for it was their support that persuaded the Millennium Commission that our small team were worth 'adopting' with a major grant, although we had to demonstrate our ability by matching them pound for pound. That we did so was in no small part due to the generosity of Redland in gifting the land so that we could count its value as a gift in kind to set against the Lottery grant, and to the decision by the National Forest to give us a major planting grant that meant we could show that work was getting underway.

We were lucky that objections by Health & Safety to our planting a visitor attraction on the first site gifted to us by Redland meant that we moved to the other bank of the River Tame before we began planting, for the new site was in every way superior to the old and Redland's wise and experienced Restoration Manager, Ron Foster, was a happier man the day we agreed the move.

One of the problems that we faced throughout this period of development was that the order of giving could not necessarily be reflected in the order of planting and recording. I had made the decision that we would wait for the trees to be established before we started allocating and labelling them. I had a fear that our early losses, which we had to expect on such a difficult site, would include many which had been dedicated and visited, and that we would create for ourselves a major problem in replacing them. Far better to wait until a healthy six year old tree showed that it was settled in and growing well. In this I was wrong, for we were frequently visited by people who had come to see their tree, only to be told that it had not been selected at that time. Eventually one of our volunteers, Bob Morris, grasped this particular bramble and not only drew up a grid by which individual trees could be monitored but undertook to tie in appropriate locations the thousands of labels that were sitting in boxes in the store room. The plan was to allocate the trees nearest to the main Service plots to those who had served in that particular branch. Aware that a thinning out process would be needed in a few years time Bob, his wife Muriel and their friend Hugh, labelled every third tree and produced maps and lists for the front of house team to show visitors where they needed to look. Even so, many of them needed to be taken out on to this vast estate to ensure that the tree was found. In this, as in so many things that required an expenditure of energy, Sue Elliott proved indefatigable, covering more miles each day than most of the rest of us put together.

The fact that we had stated at the start that this was an inclusive project and that no one who wished for a memorial tree would be turned away meant that we planted for many whom we would not have thought about at the start. One example was the Roadpeace wood where individuals who had lost their lives in traffic incidents could be commemorated. Another was the gradual taking up of trees in 'Wind in the Willows Wood' by families wishing to remember the untimely death of a youngster. On many occasions the emotions shown by individuals, either visiting privately or attending a dedication Service, were both painful and cathartic. The SANDS plot dedication, for example, was followed an hour later by a Service and tree planting in tribute to the RAF Servicing Commando. At the former, young couples wept in memory of lives that might have been, while at the latter people in their eighties wiped away tears remembering those with whom they had served and had passed on. But out of their sadness both groups expressed a joy that those whom they missed were being remembered in a most appropriate way.

The emotions of many of those attending some Services were given release by the presence of Dennis Sanders who bred white doves and who, whenever he was asked so to do, brought them to the site for release during a period of reflective silence. One could almost feel those doves bearing away on their wings the grief of the years, leaving those below like, Samson Agonistes, with 'all passions spent'.

In preparation for the Millennium tour visit by HM the Queen and the Duke of Edinburgh, Dennis had arranged for fifty doves to be bred by prisoners at Long Larton Prison as part of a rehabilitation programme. Two of the doves Dennis was very proud to have presented to the Queen to join the Royal Pigeon Loft at Sandringham. When we had proposed this part of the programme it was decided that we could not invite Her Majesty to release the doves in person in case the excitement of the occasion encouraged the birds to lighten their load on take off and in proximity to Her Majesty. The task was given to the Lord Lieutenant's Cadets once the royal group were a safe distance away and on receipt of a signal from me. I forgot. As the Queen was preparing to leave the amphitheatre she turned to me and remarked that she had not seen the doves fly off. I signalled to Dennis to release them but they did not leave their cage. 'They seem reluctant to leave,' said the Queen. 'So would you be if you had to go back to Prison,' said the Duke.

The Arboretum project also acted as a support for many of those who became involved as volunteers at the site. By its very nature the idea appealed to many who had endured conflict themselves and were now facing a future of frailty or loneliness, often having been parted from a partner of many years. Many of them found in the Arboretum and in the companionship present at the site a project which could take up their time and a purpose to which they could dedicate themselves. Few came less frequently than they felt able; many gave more time than they thought they had available. Most brought talents with them that they did not realize might be required. All who stayed gave a great deal to those around them and the visitors. The success of the project as a salve and balm could be seen in that after ten years the majority of those who had come along at the beginning were still there. For many the benefit that they gained, in addition to the joy that they gave, could be summed up in the words of Les Wills (ex- Navy and Fire Service): 'Many get involved with the Arboretum for what they can give to it; for me it was what it could give to me.'

A modest and self-effacing statement from a man who was always willing to go an extra mile and who never balked at any task. Nevertheless, the spirit of the site and its ability to share both joy and sorrow, to offer solace as well as provide delight, affected all those who were burdened. For many, it was the sharing of loss and the freedom to talk about painful experiences that they found beneficial; for some it was the discovery that, even at their age or level of infirmity, the Arboretum could offer a useful task within their capability. What mattered a great deal was that the project had no 'them' or 'us'; all those who came to help were treated, and expected to be, as equal partners whose contribution was needed.

War, so often the result of the foibles, fantasies or failures of middle aged men, so often depends for its successful execution on the fortitude and fearlessness of youth. Fitting indeed then that the most highly respected honour and award that can be presented to any individual bears the simple words 'For Valour' and has been generally presented to men who are young.

Flight Sergeant Arthur Aaron, who had already been awarded the Distinguished Flying Medal, was just 21 years old when he took off for a attack on Turin as the pilot in command of a bomber. As his plane approached the target it was hit by fire from an enemy aircraft which caused it to behave erratically. Aaron received injuries to his face and lungs and lost the use of his right arm. Nevertheless he endeavoured to remain in control of the plane and guided the bomb aimer in the hazardous task of landing the aircraft at Bone in North Africa. Nine hours after landing he died of exhaustion. His citation for the Victoria Cross reads,'In appalling conditions he showed the greatest qualities of courage, determination and leadership, and though wounded and dying, he set an example of devotion to duty which has seldom been equaled and never surpassed.' In 2002 the 218(Gold Coast) Squadron Association had a tree dedicated to Flight Sergeant Aaron planted alongside their own Squadron tree in the Arboretum.

As the idea of the Arboretum had grown from a seed planted by one of the nation's most famous and best loved holders of the Victoria Cross, Leonard Cheshire, it seemed appropriate that other Royal Air Force holders of the medal should be commemorated as well. So, along with the tree for Arthur Aaron, others were planted for: Acting Wing Commander Hughie Idwal Edwards of 105 Squadron; Squadron Leader Stewart King Scarf of 62 Squadron and Acting Wing Commander Hugh Gordon Malcolm of 18 Squadron. Each of their stories deserves to be recorded and remembered and, in time, just such a record will be available at the site. For the moment, along with Flight Sergeant Aaron, we tell the story of the South African Air Force's Captain 'Ted' Swales who flew as master bomber on a raid on Pforzheim in February 1945 and was awarded his Victoria Cross for staying at the controls of his battered and doomed aircraft until it exploded, in order that his crew could bale out successfully. Aaron, Swales and so many young airmen died in order that their crew might live; their actions recall the words from that powerful hymn of 1919, 'O Valiant Hearts' with its haunting lines:

> All you had hoped for, all you had you gave,
> To save mankind – yourself you scorned to save.

This, although frequently sung at the Arboretum, is a hymn that has been expunged from most modern Hymn Books by compilers enjoying the comforts of religious freedom thanks to the sacrifice of Swales and others, whose very deaths link them closely to the deeds of the founder of the Church to whom those compilers belong. Another group of valorous men who also performed deeds close to the great example of He whose holy work was doing good, were the army doctors who had been awarded the Victoria Cross.

It would be difficult to recall how many times the film *Zulu* has been shown on television, where it seems to have become a perennial Christmas favourite. Among the gallant band that held off the ferocious attack on the settlement at Rorke's Drift was Surgeon James Henry Reynolds who for his heroism in caring for the wounded even while under personal attack was awarded the Victoria Cross, one of 29 VCs and one George Cross awarded to members of the Royal Army Medical Corps for similar selfless bravery. Now his valour was to be remembered within the Arboretum.

It seems fitting, as a reminder that even in the furnace of conflict humanity will stand proud, that many recipients of the highest award for gallantry, including the only two people to have received the Victoria Cross twice, should have been serving with the Royal Army Medical Corps. These awards reflected the selfless courage with which they tended the wounded and endeavoured to save life while surrounded by death. And it was while planning a grove for the RAMC that the idea of honouring these very special individuals took root.

The RAMC wanted a plot where individual members of the Corps could be remembered. The logical place for this was at the far end of the Arboretum beyond 'The Beat'. Here we still had space for a large planting, and it was an area which we felt could be developed with autumn colour in mind, reflecting the purple associated with the Corps' uniform. The Avenue that stretched from the Visitor Centre to the Chetwynd Bridge over the River Tame could then be lined with Purple Beech, *Fagus sylvatica* 'Purpurea' and 'Riversii', a tree much castigated by the late Alan Mitchell but which nevertheless had a good reason to stand proud on our site. Establishing the beeches was, however, a most difficult task and a good many had to be replaced before the Avenue became established. Either side it was a different story, with the Acers and other trees which promised autumn colour growing well in ground that was a little more fertile than in most of the remainder of the site.

Yet it was not only individual holders of the Victoria Cross to whom the Arboretum was to pay tribute. The development of the site coincided with a competition to find a permanent statue to be placed on the empty plinth in Trafalgar Square, in front of the National Gallery. One of the early candidates was a sculpture of Queen Victoria on horseback awarding the first ever Victoria Cross to Mate Charles Lucas of the Royal Navy on 26 June 1857. I wrote to the VC & GC Association volunteering the Arboretum as a home for the finished work if it was not lucky enough to be selected for Trafalgar Square. In the end the full scale work was not commissioned but the artist had created a wonderful model in deep brown wax. We were offered this if we could find a suitable place to display it. Of course we could; it would stand in our central foyer where it would be seen by every visitor. The Association were delighted and provided the model with a beautiful presentation box in which to be displayed.

The day of its presentation was a most noticeable one for the Arboretum for twelve holders of the Victoria and George Cross, or their widows, were able to attend the ceremony. We were delighted but the model was not. Before very long the ambient temperature warmed up the wax and Charles Lucas leant gracefully forward until his nose rested against the flank of Queen Victoria's mount. He was returned to the upright and given more backbone but the laws of physics continued to adjust his posture until he was recast in bronze.

At that first presentation of the Victoria Cross, Queen Victoria pinned the award on the chests of 62 men, sometimes driving the pin home with such vigour that it pierced their skin and drew blood. The twenty-second recipient was Master Gunner Daniel Cambridge of the Royal Regiment of Artillery who won his award during the assault on Redan in the Crimea on 8 September 1855 when, despite several serious injuries, he not only refused to retire but ventured out under heavy fire to bring in a wounded man. Yet again, the greatest award for gallantry was bestowed on those who, disregarding the risk to their own lives, wished to save others. The grandson of Daniel Cambridge was to become involved with the Arboretum, specifically to ensure that the gallant holders of the VC and GC were remembered at the site which, at the time of writing, 144 of them were.

Fewer George Crosses are commemorated at the NMA, but included among them are the only two that were awarded to a group as opposed to an individual: the Island of Malta and the Royal Ulster Constabulary, each in their own way for bravery under siege. In the 'Y' Group plot a local hero is acknowledged, Able Seaman Colin Grazier of Tamworth, who on 30 October 1942, together with Lieutenant Tony Fasson and Canteen assistant Tommy Brown, leapt into the water from HMS *Petard*, to board the sinking *U-559* and successfully recover an Enigma Code Machine. Grazier and Fasson went down with the vessel so did not live to learn that their action had probably shortened the war by at least one year. They received posthumous George Crosses rather than Victoria Crosses, to hide the fact of their achievement from the German High Command. Sadly, the American-made film *Enigma* alters the true story for box office reasons and to hold true to the Hollywood falsehood that the Americans won the war.

The RAMC'S long list of holders of the Victoria Cross includes the youngest holder of the award, Hospital Apprentice Andrew Fitzgibbon, who was only 15 when he:

...behaved with great coolness and courage at the capture of the North Taku Fort on 21 August 1860 ... Having quitted cover he proceeded under a heavy fire, to attend to a dhoolie-bearer, whose wounds he had been directed to bind up; and while the regiment was advancing under the enemy's fire, he ran across the open to attend to another wounded man, in doing so he himself was severely wounded.

Some might consider such exemplary bravery in one so young to be in sharp contrast to another group of young men whose deaths are commemorated at the NMA, a small number of people who, for many, reflect the opposite extreme of human behaviour under fire to that displayed by holders of the Victoria Cross: those shot for cowardice or desertion in the First World War.

One such was Private Herbert Burden of the Northumberland Fusiliers. Private Burden has no known grave; neither does his name appear on any memorial to those who lost their lives in the First World War. If such a memorial existed it would record that he died at the age of nineteen on 21 July 1915. He was, in fact, seventeen, having lied about his age to enlist. Four months after his seventeenth birthday he was shot for desertion. At his tender age the slaughter at Ypres unhinged him and he deserted, only to be captured and put on trial for his life. It was a short trial and the sentence of death was unanimous. No one offered up any plea in mitigation nor was anyone available to provide a character reference.

Herbert Burden was one of 350 British and Commonwealth soldiers executed for desertion, cowardice, or other 'crimes' in the First World War. Most were young; he was probably the youngest.

When Andy de Comyn, a student sculptor, read about Private Burden he determined to use his skills to draw attention to the youngster's fate. For his graduation piece he decided to sculpt, in concrete, a larger than life size statue of the Northumberland Fusilier. But before he started he need to find somewhere to site the completed work.

In 1990, John Hipkin, who as a 15 year old merchant seaman, had been the nation's youngest prisoner of war, began a tireless campaign to have the state pardon all those who had been 'Shot at Dawn'. Intense parliamentary lobbying kept the campaign in both the public and parliament's vision but progress towards a pardon was slow. John saw that having Andy's statue on public display could only publicize his campaign so he approached the Arboretum to see if we were willing to erect it at the site.

This was quite a challenge. The Arboretum was not a campaigning organization and even were it to become one the Pardon Campaign was not necessarily one to which we could lend our voice, not least because of the offence that we might cause our many thousand of supporters. The last thing we could afford was to be boycotted for some perfectly avoidable controversy. Yet, Andy's statue was a powerful work and it did tell a poignant, if small, story. But was our site appropriate for it?

In the end I decided that it was, but we also made it clear that we took no side in the Pardons debate. This was not to avoid the issue but because it seemed to us that it was not possible to revisit the tragedy of those young men uncluttered by seventy years of progress in psychology, psychiatry, sociology and medicine and without being subject to the pressures under which those who passed judgement were operating. In simple terms, how could one group be pardoned without condemning those who had passed sentence? This conundrum was brought home at the NMA by a dedication in an entirely different part of the site: the unveiling of a plinth in tribute to all who had served on a Merchant Navy Training Ship. The organizer told me that just before his very elderly father had died he had been troubled and murmured words about, 'that poor boy'. Very disturbed, after his funeral, his family had researched his life and found out that he had been the junior member of a court martial board that had pronounced sentence of death on a young deserter. The sentence had been duly carried out, and it needs to be mentioned that only ten per cent of such sentences were, and the guilt had remained with that officer ever since. Just how appropriate the epithet 'poor boy' was can be shown by a walk down any of the row of stakes. In one the ages given are: 20, 21, 36, 32, 28, 25, 25, 26, 19, 22, 27, 20, 20, 21, 28, 20, 17, 31, 27, 20, 20, 19, 26, 23, 24. Young indeed, but walk along any row in a Commonwealth War Graves cemetery and the same range of ages will appear. War kills young men. The difference in this case is that they were shot by their own side. The insight into a very personal hell supported our contention that we could not consider ourselves in a position to be judgmental. The death of soldiers killed by their own side is an ever present tragedy of war, although these days it is the incidents of friendly fire that cause such tragic losses. Erecting the 'Shot at Dawn' statue at the Arboretum would remind visitors that nations that go to war end up in many cases killing their own – yet another reason to strive for peace.

To emphasize the tragic nature of the loss, Andy's statue, placed at the eastern end of the Arboretum where it turned pale pink with each sunrise, was not left to stand alone. In an arc behind it we placed 306 wooden stakes rising gently from the front in a series of rows reminiscent of a Greek theatre to remind the visitor that what they were looking at was a tragedy of war. Each stake was labelled with the name, rank, age and date of death of one of those who had been shot. Shortly after this, members of the public began making donations to 'adopt' a stake, funding that helped pay for the memorial and its upkeep.

The statue was unveiled in June 2001 by Gracie Harris who was three years old when her father, Harry Farr, was shot at the age of 25 in October

1916. Private Farr had already been evacuated suffering from shell shock and returned to the lines but when he reported sick and refused to advance in September he was court martialled and sentenced to death for desertion without any further medical examination. His daughter Gracie did not find out about his fate until she was 40, so had no idea of the pain her mother had to bear. Her remarks and those of other relatives were eagerly sought after on the day of the unveiling, which attracted intense media interest. Interviews began at 0600 and continued well into the evening, with one radio channel running a two hour phone-in on the rights or wrongs of erecting such a tribute. The majority were in favour but no views counted as much as those of a bemedalled centenarian who stood proudly to attention as the statue was unveiled and stated that those who saw wrong in the idea did not understand the issue as he did, for he 'had been there'.

Unrelated to the whole 'Shot at Dawn' issue was a tree planted some distance away bearing the simple, sad label;

> Percy James Wise, joined aged 16, wounded at the Somme, discharged for neglect due to shell shock; placed in mental institute and died 2 September 1964.

Until and unless we can state we are comfortable with the treatment of young men like Percy Wise then we cannot sit as judge and jury over those, many of them suffering similar strains, who abandoned their posts and were shot for so doing.

At the annual National Service Veterans Service in June 2006 I had the opportunity to walk down to the 'Shot at Dawn' statue with Andy de Comyn and the Minister for Veterans Affairs, Tom Watson. Knowing that the Minister was shortly to make a statement to the House on the issue of pardons, I had wanted to show him how we at the Arboretum had handled the issue. Tom Watson listened sympathetically and was very interested in the conundrum of pardoning without giving offence or casting retrospective judgement on those who had passed sentence. We struck a common chord and it was gratifying when, a few weeks later, the Minister announced that pardons would be issued; the concerns we had voiced were also covered in a most sympathetic statement. Gratifying also was the fact that *The Daily Telegraph* put the story on its front page and illustrated it with a large photograph of the state of Private Burden.

Not all the individuals for whom we planted a tree had a direct link with conflict although, given that the NMA paid homage to the whole of a wartime generation, most of our plantings commemorated someone whose life had been touched by war, such as those who were remembered in a wonderful arc of bloom alongside the Darbyshire Ditch.

Among our local business supporters was the Midlands Co-operative Society whose Director of Corporate Affairs, Peter Vaughan, was determined to be involved with the project in as many ways as was possible. One day he brought along the Director of their Funeral Services and we discussed a scheme whereby people arranging a funeral service through the Co-op could have a memorial tree planted at the site. I had long wished to create a riot of Spring blossom at the Arboretum and if we could do so as a celebration of life it seemed a good way of achieving it, for the idea of Spring blossom with its links to new life and hope seemed to marry the idea of paying tribute in celebration of a life well lived and for hope beyond grief. The response, yet again, was overwhelming and each year we added another row of trees until we had to declare the site full. But until then we held a service of dedication for all those who had asked for trees to be planted in the previous twelve months. As the numbers attending were too great to fit into the Chapel, the Service was held in the Visitor Centre Hall before families walked down to the site to see their loved one's tree for the first time. Walking among them at this time was another emotional moment at the site. At the end everyone trooped back to eat a tasty picnic lunch provided by Midlands Co-operative; a very successful venture. In accordance with our desire that the Arboretum be a place of joy this whole large section of woodland was called the 'Celebration of Life' plot, for the trees in their blossoming glory are there both to pay tribute to a loved one and to celebrate and bring back memories of a life lived together. Labels chosen at random on trees throughout the Arboretum reflect that ode to the joy of knowing and loving someone:

> Remembering happy woodland walks with
> a beloved Father, Norman Turner

> Barbara F Williams,
> WRVS Meals Organiser.
> The smile we loved to be remembered forever,
> love, kindness, friendship, bravery beyond
> endurance.

> Captain Douglas Howard Gautrey
> whose Christian beliefs and thoughts of dearest wife 'Bey'
> surmounted and survived his POW privations.

> Albert Edward Tibble, Civil Defence,
> killed in an air raid, 21 December 1942
> and his widow Dora Annie Tibble.
> badly injured 21 December 1942,

A very courageous and loving mother,
a tree seems just right for her memory.

Peter Vaughan was also responsible for funding another significant stretch of woodland that ran alongside the River Tame. We wanted to recreate along this bank the original riverine wood that would have grown here before farming moved along the valley thousands of years ago and chopped or burnt down the forest, giving to the area such names as Burntwood. This would also be an opportunity to plant the threatened Black Poplar, *Populus nigra* var. *betulifolia*, a magnificent example of which grew on the opposite bank. But first we started with willow, which we invited local schools to come along to help us plant.

One raw December day with a gale driving in from the north one of the school teachers looked up and said, 'Shouldn't we call this "Wind in the Willows Wood" for it's very windy and we're planting willow?' Within thirty second she had an answer and the wood a new name. When the Essex Woodcarvers were told this they said, 'Goody, goody, Ratty and Moley', and in due course these carved animals appeared, along with Toad, Badger and two Weasels for, given the origins of the wood, it was always going to be a one linked to children. This makes it one of the sadder sites of the NMA, for many of the children to whom trees have been dedicated are those who have died in infancy or their early years. It gives it not even a tenuous link with the main aim of the site but the spirit of the site meant that we had to 'suffer little children to come and forbid them not' – who would act differently?

The NMA project had begun by working with two mutually exclusive types of land use – gravel extraction and forestry. However, we had been shown, mainly by Ron Foster of Redland, how these two elements could be considered to be mutually advantageous. Then in the Spring of 2001 we were made aware of an individual who had combined both of them in his working life.

Professor Derek Lovejoy, a landscape architect of international repute, had worked with the Sand and Gravel Association and influenced the way in which exhausted sites could be reclaimed to maximise the public benefit once the aggregate companies had moved on. He had also been a Chairman of the Tree Council and the International Tree Foundation, both of which were involved with the NMA. So when his daughter wrote to ask whether we would be able to plant a memorial wood for her father, it seemed logical to say 'yes'. The only problem was, once again, the lack of space at the site. However, I was trying to build up the courage to plant beyond the railway embankment on the triangle of land enclosed between it and the banks of the river Tame and Trent. The desire for a Derek Lovejoy Wood forced that decision upon us and took the Arboretum to its logical eastern boundary.

CHAPTER NINE

The Poppy Tree:
A Vision for the Future

A beech, a cedar, and a lime
Grow on my lawn, embodying time.
A lime, a cedar, and a beech
The transience of this lifetime teach.
Beech, cedar, lime, when I'm dead Me,
You'll stand, lawn-shadowing, tree by tree;
And in your greenery, while you last,
I shall survive who shared your past.

Siegfried Sassoon

Unlike the majority of our fellow countrymen and the Millennium Commission, we at the NMA had always held to the conviction that the new Millennium would begin at the start of 2001. Although this might have been a correct interpretation of the calendar it was also to our advantage to hold to this belief. Our builders had gone bankrupt and we had lost over six months while legal issues were hammered out before work could continue. Opening in 2001 suited us admirably. Even so there would be areas of the site, including that between the Visitor Centre and the Chapel, that would not be completed, but we truly believed that one of our strengths was that visitors would be able to return again and again and watch the site develop. 'Be a witness to creation' was the phrase that we used, while at the same time emphasising just how long it took young trees to get established. Still by May 2001 the building complex, which was the part funded by the Millennium Commission, was sure to be finished. So, after discussions with out Patron, the Duchess of Kent, 16 May was selected as the date for the official opening.

The Duchess was a most relaxed and approachable royal. Delighted with providing a forward to the souvenir programme, she declined the offer of having a speech drafted for her since she wished to speak off the cuff following her tour of the site from which she would gain her own views on what was of importance. Neither did she wish for accommodation to be arranged on her behalf, preferring a short list of hotels in the area from which she could make a choice and her own booking.The week ahead of the visit was filled with May showers making the site very wet underfoot. Luckily a local company had loaned us two open-sided rough terrain vehicles which could take the Duchess and VIPs around to the various memorial plots. So, following a short service in the Chapel, we embarked in these boat-like structures and drove around, stopping at as many plots as possible to talk to the groups gathered at each one. Sadly, time and the threatening skies meant that not every plot was visited, and there were several disappointed individuals. Nevertheless, when the Duchess gave her extemporary speech, she delighted all who heard her talk with obvious delight at the occasion and joy, as the daughter of a forester, at seeing so much meaningful planting. With good media coverage of the whole day, we were delighted to open the next day to receive a number of visitors who had only been made aware of our existence by that coverage. Now came the anxiety of waiting to see if subsequent visitor numbers would keep the project viable.

With the Arboretum having been opened officially it was now time to turn to its long-term future. Early indications were that we were reaching our modest visitor number targets, but the money being raised from visitors was not, for several years to come, going to enable us to do much more than care for and maintain what we had on site. We knew there were still many areas that needed bringing up to the standard that would be expected of a site claiming a very important national role. That role and the way we met it also needed looking at, for we were a very small team responsible for an extremely important and sensitive function that could not be delivered if, for example, our existence was not known by a large majority of people throughout the country. Yet we had no marketing arm and no support from either the Government or other significant national organisations. We were a coracle with a precious cargo that would not be spotted on the rough waters in which we tried to stay afloat. At any time we could be run down by a mightier vessel or even made redundant by a new initiative. In a short time all these concerns became focussed around linked issues of entry and ownership.

Our entry charges were modest, but this did not mean that those at reception were not confronted by visitors annoyed that they were being asked to pay to see a tree that they had paid for or which was linked to a unit in which they had served. Most, but by no means all, accepted our explanation that we were a charity that needed money to pay for maintenance, services and salaries. Nevertheless, those visitors were making a good point: should we, as custodians of memorials to those who had served their country, be charging those who came to pay tribute to their lives? Were we offering a benefit or providing a service? That might seem to be merely semantics, but it could have been a very expensive issue.

One day we received a letter from the local VAT office stating that they had paid a visit to the site, walked around, looked at the memorials and decided that we owed some £268,000 in VAT. For what? Their view was that every individual or group who had dedicated a tree was receiving a benefit, and therefore the transaction was subject to VAT. This was serious. We did not have a spare £268, let alone £268,000. Luckily, one of our Trustees, Sir Henry Every, was a partner at Deloitte and Touche and they kindly volunteered to go in to bat on our behalf *pro bono*. This led to several lengthy meetings and numerous letters during which issues were debated such as whether or not a small brass memorial label on a Chapel chair or a dedicatory Bakelite tally on a tree provided a benefit. We even had to have arcane discussions as to who was the beneficiary of a memorial that had been created for an organisation which no longer existed. After months of discussion the local Customs & Excise had not budged one inch. If they continued with their demand, we told them, the Arboretum would have to close down. They did not waiver.

There seemed to be only one option left. Our local Member of Parliament, the eccentric and maverick Michael Fabricant, had been a supporter of the Arboretum from the start and attended several of our events. He had also gone in to bat, successfully, on a similar issue for a Royal Marines memorial in London. I felt sure that he could help us but needed to provide him with some ammunition. I felt that the local VAT team had given us just that.

During our discussions I had raised the matter of the Northern Ireland Ash Grove. Here we had planted trees for each Serviceman murdered during the 'Troubles,' a project that had received generous support from the Northern Ireland Office. However, we had offered the families of those killed the opportunity to place a small memorial plaque, manufactured by Blinford Graphics, beside their loved one's tree at a cost of £100. This small contribution was one of the items that the Inspectors insisted was liable to VAT. This above all else made me see red. The Government had required these young men to put their lives in danger, to die for their country, and yet when, at no expense to the Exchequer a memorial was created in tribute to them, the treasury wished to benefit by £17.50 for every life lost. This was the right ammunition for Michael Fabricant who could now add personal incensement to our cry of 'foul play'. Within a week he had called upon the Minister and shown him how ludicrous and wrong the situation was. Moreover, he pointed out, publicising the fact would not prove beneficial to the Government. One week later two senior

VAT Inspectors from London came to see us. We walked them around, and although they seemed most interested in the site they did not ask any of the questions that I had anticipated, seeming content just to enjoy a nice stroll around the site on a sunny day. By the time we got back to sit down for discussions I was very nervous.

One of them flourished a leaflet that we had available at the front desk which explained how individuals could have a dedicatory tree planted. How many people had taken advantage of this? It was a relatively new form – ten at the most had taken up the offer. The Inspector explained that the wording clearly indicated that a benefit was being bestowed, and such transactions were subject to VAT. They left, charming throughout but with no indication of their thoughts. A week later we received a copy of a letter from the Central Region Appeals Team which stated:

> The disputed assessment for £268,000 was issued on 27 February 2001 and concerned undeclaration of tax in VAT period 02/98 to 11/00. As a result of negotiations, and using the figures provided … this assessment should now be reduced to £88. However, for administrative convenience for both your clients and Customs & Excise, I can confirm that this amount is to be withdrawn in full.

I contacted Michael Fabricant who informed me that, following his meeting, the Minister had instructed the Senior VAT Inspectors to visit our site and only return when they had a solution that was acceptable to both parties. An excellent MP, and a wise Minister.

Although the VAT settlement was a reprieve it left us no better off and we still needed to raise money to cover our costs. Strangely, it was far harder to interest donors in revenue income than it had been to gain support for the capital works. The general view was that if one could not support one's ongoing costs through income then one was not a going concern and thus not worth any investment. We had to search around for other activities to attract funds. Thus it was that at the age of over fifty I found myself taking part in two London marathons; a painful pleasure that covered several weeks of running costs.

Some of these costs had not been anticipated. Within a few months of opening, the Visitor Centre had been broken into four times during the night by someone who had worked out that we were so isolated that, even should there be an immediate response to our alarms, there would be enough time to get away with any haul. Luckily, all our cash was removed from the site at night and little of value was taken, but boarded up windows did not give a good impression. We were forced to employ night watchmen, an unforeseen and major monthly cost. After a few months we moved away from contract watch keepers to employing them ourselves and including the overnight cleaning tasks amongst their responsibilities. Far from finding this onerous, the night watchmen welcomed the additional duty as it helped pass the time and kept them awake. However, the cost still meant that we porpoised around the zero balance line on our bank account, keeping afloat by occasional injections of the oxygen of unexpected income. To grow sturdily like our trees we needed to be secured to a stronger stake.

The VAT incident made us think through the whole issue of costs and charges. It seemed wrong that the NMA was providing a service to the nation that acknowledged a national debt, but was charging people to pay that homage which the nation itself need to be reminded of. Surely, and ideally, we should have free entry in a similar way to that available at the major national museums and galleries. The MoD had a grant-in-aid budget and I called on the Department that ran this to see if we could put a case forward for support. The immediate answer was, 'No,' based on the principle, one which I fully understood, that the MoD did not pay for memorials. At first that seemed to be both illogical and indefensible, but when one considered what constituted a memorial and the number that might spring up if funding was available it was very easy to see and accept the Ministry's position. Nonetheless, I felt that the Arboretum was not in this position; we were not asking for construction costs but custodial ones. Progress was slow and then, strangely, the solution came from the very same office within the very same Department when it was announced by the Secretary of State for Defence that the Armed Forces Memorial was to be built at the NMA.

I had awaited his decision so that I could return to the matter of entry charges. The VAT affair had shown how sensitive the issue could be, but now we had a situation where the nation was going to place a most significant memorial at a location where those who wished to pay tribute would have to pay for the right to do so. I made myself a nuisance once again at the MoD and came away with a provisional promise from John Sinfield, the Civil Service head of the relevant department, that grant-in-aid to allow free entry would be forthcoming provided two other caveats were met. These were, confirmation that the Armed Forces Memorial was to be erected on the site, and agreement over future ownership of the NMA which had always been a major concern of mine.

From early on it was apparent that this nationally significant site required the infrastructure support of an established national organisation if it were to face its future with confidence. There could be little doubt that once the trees had matured it would be a great visitor attraction, and once we had gained the Armed Forces Memorial and grant-in-aid we would be in a far better situation than we might have been, but we still needed more professional support than we could afford to market the site and to provide the comfort of deeper pockets.

There were, in my opinion, three possible partners: the National Forest, Forest Enterprise and the Royal British Legion (TRBL). The National Forest had its own visitor attraction in Conkers and saw its role as a supporter of other landowners in the area not as an acquirer of its own estate. Forest Enterprise, with its excellent Arboretum at Westonbirt and its pinetum at Bedgebury, was a most willing provider of advice and stock but not in a position to take on another attraction. Either of these might have been appropriate if we considered ourselves to be an Arboretum that had a memorial role, but we were really a Memorial in the form of an Arboretum. We grew remembrance in the form of trees and our key task was to provide a place appropriate for that duty and that debt. I felt from the start that TRBL was our logical partner.

They had been involved from the pre-planting days. Through Charles Lewis we had received much advice and support and we had worked closely with him in the campaign to reintroduce the national observance of the two-minute silence every 11 November. In support of this the Legion had attended at both local, county and national level every one of our Armistice Day Services. They had even printed the Order of Service. Glancing at the first one, the attendance of the National Vice-Chairman, National Chairman and Vice Chairman of the Women's Section along with the past Chairman and Treasurer are recorded. The Legion also provided buglers from the Central Band to play Last Post and Reveille. Subsequent Orders of Service show the same level of attendance. Two of those attending deserve special mention: the Women's Chairman, Mrs Mary Arnold, who organised the commissioning of the altar frontal as a gift from her ladies, and Mrs Maureen Cole, who was to become National Women's Chairman and who attended our service year after year

In the original plan for the site I had intended to plant a Royal British Legion poppy field but this became too difficult to lay down in the formative years. Instead, a number of RBL branches planted trees on the ridge that separated the site from the gravel works and, as this was also the direction from which the prevailing wind blew, they served a double purpose.

Locally, we had received a great deal of support from the Chairman of the Alrewas Branch, Derek Hopkins and his wife Marie. Not only had they provided a great deal of hospitality at their well laid out and organised Club, but their members also turned out to help with the directing of traffic and car parking for major events. What we needed to do was turn these links into a formal partnership. Charles Lewis had always been in favour but he was moving on, leaving me with an entirely new team with whom to negotiate.

Our argument was very strong. We were a brand new initiative that could remind the nation of its duty of remembrance every day of the year, not just in November. Moreover we were doing so in such a way that appealed not just to members of the wartime generations but to youngsters who enjoyed learning about their debt to the past in this way. Properly developed we would grow, along with our trees, to be the place where the nation gathered, either as a whole or as specific groups, to pay tribute in a way that would not grow old but would live and flourish and delight generations to come. Few would have contested the strength of that argument or disagreed that, now the Legion had added 'Remembrance' to its objectives, we were an ideal way in which they could deliver that function on behalf of the nation. However, for the Legion to take us on they needed to be sure that we were not a potentially costly liability. Simply put, I was offering a present, but were they being sold a pup?

I did not think so. The first few years of opening when we had to convert capital income to revenue income were always going to be hard. We had had our lucky break. One day I collected a letter redirected from the World Memorial Fund's old London address. It was from the executors of the will of a Mrs Went who had left WMF over a quarter of a million pounds. This was not the first letter in an exchange of correspondence which had taken place between the solicitors and WMF's old treasurer, Jonathan Brown, who had decided that Mrs Went's wishes would best be realised if all the money was passed on to the Leonard Cheshire Chair of Conflict Recovery which, since we had initiated its absorption by Leonard Cheshire did not need the funds as much as did the Arboretum, the other offspring of WMF. A series of urgent and at times acrimonious conversations took place, at the end of which I asked WMF's old Trustees to make a judgement. They agreed to split the legacy in two equal shares. The £100,000 that the Arboretum received could not have come at a more critical moment. Bless Mrs Went.

Once the legacy had been paid, the Arboretum was able to sort out several issues mainly concerning the setting up of the kitchens and catering facilities. We had thought that our brand new project might attract a young team keen to establish their own restaurant business. We had some ideas as to what we wanted to see, for example, I was keen that the produce of trees should be a theme running through the menu. This was easier to do starting with desserts and working back. Thus puddings could be based around orange sorbet, lemon meringue, date, almond slices, chocolate coconut ice and a lot more besides. Starters would include avocado. It was the main course that would be the most difficult, although flaked almonds and the ubiquitous vegetarian nut cutlet, cunningly transformed into an object of desire, would cover this along with the use of pine nuts and pesto. What we most desired was a team who could bring inspiration to this idea, but we could not find them. We tried through the local catering schools and also the Prince's Trust but in the end gave the franchise to a group who were prepared to be involved in a venture of which few had heard, in an isolated country location. It worked. Although there were teething troubles we had just one occasion where a meal was not to standard, and the story of catering at the Arboretum was a savoury and wholesome one. Although the various chefs deserve credit, the people who made it work were the staff, volunteers and 'Friends' who acted as waiters, sandwich makers, washers up and clearers away. Many a crisis was kept from the guests by frantic conversations and changes of plan behind the scenes, while a calm appearance belied the panic. By the time that the Arboretum approached the Royal British Legion the catering was well established and profitable.

The site itself was, of course, youthful. Barry Jones had established a grass cutting and tree maintenance regime which, month after month, showed improvements, so that more and more return visitors were heard to comment that they could not believe how much better things looked. Barry and his assistant Dave Worsley developed a slick routine to prepare for dedicatory tree planting, so that every visiting group was made to feel that their tree was as special to us as it was to them. We were helped in this respect by our royal visits. For the opening we had purchased a special spade for the Duchess of Kent to plant her tree and we had another for Her Majesty the Queen and the Duke of Edinburgh. In addition, for the latter visit PAMAL, a Midlands garden furniture manufacturer, had presented us with two inscribed planting boxes in which the soil to be placed around the trees was kept, making the ceremonial planting more of a special event. Barry then ensured that these boxes and spades were present at all subsequent plantings; a small matter but one that was much appreciated by every group.

The decision by the Lord Lieutenant, James Hawley, to suggest that the Arboretum be included on the Queen's schedule for her millennium visit to Staffordshire came at the time when we were sounding out TRBL on a joined up future. The Legion itself had not planned its own millennium event at that time so were delighted to accept our offer of making Her Majesty's visit their main celebratory occasion. It was to be the largest event staged so far at the site and the staff and expertise that the Legion were able to bring to bear on the occasion was impressive. As always, the management of the occasion was undertaken by Jackie Fisher with her increasingly experienced and numerous team of 'Friends' and established contacts, augmented by loan personnel from TRBL. Marquees and beer tents, caterers and a band, were all organised by the Legion under Russell Thompson's direction, and the Legion also coordinated the involvement of several hundred standard bearers who were to form a most impressive circle of honour fallen in at the top of the Leonard Cheshire amphitheatre. We had also invited local school children and our wood carvers, while the

County had several of its own millennium initiatives that they wished the Queen to see brought to the site. On the day the site bulged and we were lucky that many of the close-in plots, such as the War Widows' Rose Garden, had not been planted or else we would have had nowhere to place the guests.

The Duke of Edinburgh arrived first and, seeing the Corps of Drums of the Staffordshire Army Cadets near by, sidestepped the meeters and greeters and went off to talk to the cadets before falling into line as Her Majesty arrived. As always on these occasions, there was a long line of local dignitaries whom Her Majesty had to meet, but on this occasion every one of them was involved with the creation of the Arboretum or its future. It was also an opportunity to introduce many members of the 'Friends' to the Queen, a small but important acknowledgement of the work that they had put in to turn a dream into reality.

The visit also gave us the chance to involve other groups who had given us so much of their time: the Lichfield Cathedral Mobile Belfry, the Band of RAF Cosford, the Sutton Coldfield Sea Cadets, and the Essex Woodcarvers as well as our local school children. Many of the latter had come with posies or pictures of the Queen that they had drawn themselves. She accepted every one offered up to her, bending down to thank each small donor. The support arrangements were remarkable. Although she accepted hundreds of gifts she never had more than two in her hand at any one time, Lady Farnham and the Lord Lieutenant's Cadets managing a slick relay back to the car.

The formal part of the visit was centred around a short service in the Chapel whose large glass doors were wide open so that the congregation seated in and around the amphitheatre could join in. It was the first time that we had filled the amphitheatre, and the participation of those gathered under the clear blue sky and in sight of our trees made the occasion very special indeed. On completion of the service Her Majesty and the Duke of Edinburgh stepped outside for the playing of the National Anthem which was accompanied by the lowering of a circle of standards, the sight of which added to the 'not a dry eye' events in the Arboretum.

The Queen and the Duke then separated and walked to the corners of the amphitheatre where they each planted a golden beech, *Fagus sylvatica* 'Dawyck Gold'. The choice of this particular upright tree was based around a hope that the millennium celebrations might herald the dawn of an 'age of gold' and the recollection that some years earlier our first major public event at the Arboretum was a planting in celebration of the Queen and the Duke's Golden Wedding, at which the Duke of Kent made the first of his several visits to the site. Rather tardily these two golden trees celebrated that anniversary as well.

This was a cheerful note on which to end what had been both a successful visit and a demonstration to the RBL of just what the Arboretum meant and was capable of becoming. The fact that the day had not only run smoothly but been fun as well was much commented on by the Legion representatives even before, with the royal party departed, the band of the Prince of Wales's Division (Clive) had stopped playing a medley of nostalgic tunes, and certainly before Legion members had drunk the beer tent dry. Sadly, the hope for a peaceful new millennium symbolised by the nationwide celebrations was finally overthrown by the events of 9/11 and the invasions of both Afghanistan and Iraq. The NMA's duty of remembrance was going to be owed to the future as well as the past.

Following the Royal Visit, talks about handing the site over to the Legion began in earnest. Although their National Executive had expressed their enthusiasm and voted to go ahead, their staff were determined to check that the Legion was not taking on a liability. The legal basis for site acquisition was studied in detail, revealing that a lot had been done through gentlemen's agreements that now needed to be signed up: we had, for example, planted on more land than the documents indicated had been granted to us, which, although it had kept our momentum up, was not an entirely satisfactory state of affairs for the new owner. Bit by bit the legal niceties were sorted out while at the same time the future viability of the site was discussed in great detail. The MoD decision to award grant-in-aid was going to be a great help but that had been awarded with the caveat that it depended on the RBL taking over the site. The RBL, on the other hand, was not prepared to take on the Arboretum without either the grant or the presence of the Armed Forces Memorial which itself needed the grant-in-aid. Months of tail chasing ensued, almost reaching the stage of each party waiting for the other to blink first. A favourable outcome was, in my opinion, inevitable, but progress was slow. There was also disagreement at the Arboretum as to the best way to proceed.

The Arboretum's Trustees wanted nothing more than a quick resolution of the takeover so that they could move on. Some of them believed that the best way to achieve this was to tell TRBL that our future was precarious and that, without the Legion's support, we would cease to be a going concern. This was not so. Our Business Plan had been written as pessimistically as possible to ensure that we did not, like some Millennium projects, base a rosy future upon unrealisable visitor numbers. As long as our numbers grew, or grant-in-aid was forthcoming, the Arboretum would grow slowly but securely like many of our trees. The Legion were faced, therefore, with contrasting information depending on whom they spoke to. In the end I do not believe that they would have agreed to the deal if they considered the Arboretum to be a potential drain on their own resources.

The amalgamation process caused me some personal difficulties. As far as the site was concerned, although its main focus was on tributes to those who had served with the armed and merchant service, there were a number of plots dedicated to civilian organisations, the care of which would fall outside the Legion's remit. I had proposed that, because most of these included members of the wartime generation who had served in or supported our forces, then they could be embraced as a whole. However, there were plots such as the SANDS or Roadpeace ones where even to attempt such a link would have been disingenuous. At one time the Legion proposed removing these anomalies, but the potential siting of the Armed Forces Memorial at the site convinced the proponents of that drastic step that the balance would remain firmly one that retained its aim to be the nation's focus for all year round remembrance.

Up to this moment the Arboretum had been created and run by a small group of local people who had become close and willing friends, able to bring their own talents and ideas to the project and knowing that their input would always be discussed and adopted if valuable. The same applied to our hundreds of plot sponsors who, if they had any problems, knew that either Jackie or I would be willing to listen sympathetically and take remedial action. Among this large group there grew a major concern that we would be sacrificing local decision taking and involvement for distant faceless bureaucracy. A number of meetings were necessary to convince the doubters that amalgamation with TRBL was our best and most appropriate way forward. And so it proved to be. Most of the staff, and most importantly Jackie Fisher, stayed on so that, for the visitors, no administrative changes were noticeable. What was going to be noticeable were improvements to the site, for the security of having the Legion as its owners meant tasks that could not at that time be undertaken until funds had been raised, always a slow process, could be commissioned with confidence. The Legion takeover not only guaranteed the future, it delivered a better site.

There was, however, to be no role for me in the new arrangements. The site needed a professional on-site Director, a position that I could not fulfil, and I did not feel that the new appointee would want me hovering in the background to potentially advise and criticise. With TRBL in place, with grant-in-aid being paid and with the Armed Forces Memorial being located at the site, I had achieved what I had set out to do. With any project there is a time to go, and this was probably mine. I had always aimed at handing the project on to the RBL and had wished them to see it as a gift. It was, in fact, by now a very valuable asset which was being freely given, which seemed to be a reasonable description of a gift. However, for understandable reasons, TRBL had approached the deal as a takeover, viewing any rosy sales pitch as suspect propaganda. This had led to some discord, mainly based around my inability to provide written evidence of many different agreements that we had in place. There was little standardisation since most groups had wanted special factors taken into account. I had not produced a standard *pro forma* laying out agreed liabilities and commitments and, most importantly, I had not committed any group to ongoing support for maintenance of their sites. At the time, I had seen these *ad hoc* arrangements as the best way to ensure the maximum number of groups became involved in what was a nascent initiative from which all of them could have walked away. As a new project we had needed their involvement more than they had needed us. Now we were established, those numerous arrangements needed to be codified. My gift may have been wrapped nicely but it was held together by numerous hidden pins.

Throughout 2006 and 2007 the Armed Forces Memorial took shape. In a way its final form was dictated by the low lying nature of the one space available, which meant that, if visitors were not sometimes going to have to wade to it, the memorial needed to be raised above the flood plain. The result was a great tumulus that would command but not dominate the Arboretum site. This huge memorial mound calls to mind that raised so long ago over Leonidas's Spartans or, in more recent times, the great tumulus at Waterloo. Between those two events it also recalls a green hill far away where in the words of the veterans' hymn:

Christ, our Redeemer, went the self same way.

One can reach the summit either by walking up a straight flight of steps or by a spiral path that winds between the mound and a number of evergreen holm oaks that like green sentinels guard the memorial. The best is to climb up in hope and return the longer way where the views of the surrounding Arboretum and Staffordshire countryside give the visitor an outlook over a countryside at peace and time to reflect on what they have just seen and been a part of, for the memorial on the summit demands our involvement.

The first thing one notices as one walks between two tall concentric circular walls of Portland stone is that one is cut off from the world outside. There is no distraction, it is as if one had been placed within a soundproof room, open to the sky, in which an energy of sorts was about to focus all its strength on one's puny form made insignificant by the surrounding beige cliffs of stone. And then one notices a group of figures on either side standing against the walls. They are larger than life, which adds to one's feeling of having shrunk, and they are for the most part cast in heroic form, which makes one feel even smaller. What they symbolise is the pity and the pain of war. And, standing as they do, they invite, no force, one to be a part of that pity. The first group depicts four men carrying, with raised arms, a colleague on a stretcher while a weeping woman and distraught child look on. The still figure raised heavenward by the bearers reflects both loss, dignity and sacrifice. He could almost be an offering to the gods. Whatever one's personal interpretation, gazing at the group one is transcended beyond the indignity of war to a plain on which the strife is over. The way the four men are united in their common purpose also calls to mind the famous sculpture of the American soldiers raising the flag at Iwo Jima, but this group is not based on any one particular incident. It is outside the bourne of time and place. It even harks back to Patroclus being hoisted up above the strife in front of the walls of Troy to be carried back to the Greek camp, or other warriors being brought home upon their shields; while the mother witnessing the scene could be white-armed Andromache grieving as the lifeless Hector is carried into Troy. Why look back that far? There are many portrayals of Christ being brought down from the cross before his weeping mother that come to mind as well. The work has both a timelessness and an inclusiveness that are the proud attributes of all great memorials. Part of our duty to our dead and those that mourn their loss is to show not only that they did not die in vain but that in death they have become part of an army that no man can number, whose sacrifice was a necessary requirement of the land that they loved and will be honoured for all time. What better way to show that this honour is eternal than by linking it back into the mists of time?

On the opposite wall a naked, lifeless corpse is being tended by a woman in service uniform whose raw emotions and sweaty hair in the heat and grime of war are plainly apparent. Beside her and showing a similar compassion, is a Gurkha soldier representing not only that brave and loyal regiment but standing for the many ethnic backgrounds that united to form Britain's armed forces. Behind them, balanced on an ammunition box, a sculptor, having witnessed the scene, chisels into the stone 'We Will Remember Them, Today, Tomorrow and Forever.' This linking of the moment of death in the heat of combat with the duty of remembrance, making the warriors the composers of their own memorial, is a brilliant touch, for it unites those who die with those who live, and the chiselled words become not just a commandment but a codicil. Perhaps those words could have been 'Remember Us ...'. In any case, they call to mind another duty: 'Do this in Remembrance of Me.'

The fourth figure of this southern group is concentrating on something beyond the pity of war. He stands beside a small opening in a large pair of doors which is lined up with a similar slot in the outside wall. At eleven o' clock on the eleventh of November the sun shines through this gloomy portal and a shaft of light kindles the altar in the centre between the two groups of figures. Immortal life or even, for the unbeliever, a light to show that despite the loss and pain and sorrow and despair, life has a spark that will never be extinguished. Yet again, ancient references spring appropriately to life. One thinks of that great mound on Orkney, Maes Howe, down whose lengthy shaft the setting sun on midwinter day casts a beam. 'Lift up your eyes', the figure at the Arboretum seems to say 'the light will not fail'. With this in mind, one's eyes return to the naked corpse and the reason for his noble nakedness becomes obvious. We are being taken forward to the day of the last trump when all shall be raised, complete and whole, the mutilation of war no more apparent. From old church wall paintings to Stanley Spencer this triumph over death has been depicted across the globe in the universal hope that one day suffering shall be no more and that death will have no more dominion. The figure at the Arboretum is triumphing at the very moment of death. One cannot fail to be uplifted.

Although the figures have no truck with the vainglory of war, the way that they have been cast by the sculptor, Ian Rank-Broadley, makes them glorious in themselves not just because of their heroic proportions and physique, but in the tasks that they are carrying out. He has succeeded in showing the care, compassion, comradeship and greater qualities present in the men and women whose 16,000 names are recorded on the enclosing walls.

The list seems endless, as year after year, by Service and in alphabetical order, the names and initials of those who have died on active duty are deeply incised into the stone. There are no ranks here, all are equal through what they gave, but together they form a distinguished and never to be forgotten army united in sacrifice. Many of the friends and relatives who attended the opening service were to remark that two things gave them comfort on the day. The first was to meet with others who had gone through the same dark valley of loss as they had themselves and to realise that they did not grieve alone; the second was, in reading that so familiar name on the memorial linked with so many others, the realisation that, whatever the circumstances surrounding their death, their loved one too was not alone. They drew comfort from reading the names above and below their special one and it mattered not to them, they did not enquire or wish to know, whether those people listed so close in death were corporals or colonels, Catholics or Protestants, Muslims or Jews, agnostics or atheists, for in death they were not divided.

The Armed Forces Memorial, through its design and the materials used, provides another important link. The list of names carved simply on Portland stone recalls similar memorials such as the Royal Naval memorial at Portsmouth, while the dignified simplicity of the names links it with the many rows of names at Thiepval and Ypres. The losses may have been fewer and the battles of less renown, but the names of those lost now live forever with those from the greater conflagrations. Although one is surrounded by the human cost of war the memorial uplifts the spirit and encourages visitors to lift up their eyes. This is not only evident in the shaft of light but in the final element, the tall obelisk which the architect,

Liam O'Connor, has placed at the east end of the memorial with its gold-covered top. Mention has been made of the shaft of light from the eleven o'clock sun but the exhortation from Laurence Binyon's poem 'For the Fallen' states:

> At the going down of the sun and in the morning,
> We will remember them.

Few are able to be on that green hill at dawn and dusk on the 11 November but those that can will see the obelisk coated in a glorious pink light while its burnished point glistens, directing the watcher towards the heavens.

Only one thing chills in this tribute to the dead. The names run out and blank ahead of them stretch panels on which a further 15,000 can be recorded. It is up to us all to strive to see that far fewer are chiselled here than have gone before.

The opening of the Armed Forces Memorial by Her Majesty The Queen on 12 October 2007 was a significant moment not only for the nation but for the NMA as well. On that day the project could finally claim that it had earned its name and was now established as the nation's year round centre of remembrance. The vision was now a reality.

That early vision is now is being delivered by the Royal British Legion on behalf of all the thousands of people who put their fath in the idea of planting a living tribute to those who gave so much so that we could all enjoy a future walking among the greenwood trees in peace.

Epilogue

Plant here, for other eyes, that kingly tree
Whose reign we shall not see.
Choose well the spot, that other eyes may bless
Its natural loveliness.
Let them not guess what loving pains we took,
Or how we paused to look
From every knoll and every vantage ground
In all the landscape round,
That one invisible tree one day shall fill
Its place upon the hill.
Give to our vanished thoughts its perfect form,
And stand against the storm,
Playing its own true parts, when we are gone,
For you my little son.

Alfred Noyes

Remember the Future

A Service for Tree Sunday (November)

ORDER OF SERVICE

Welcome

In 1934, in response to a broadcast appeal, a decision was made to link Armistice Day, the 11th November, with a nationwide day of tree planting.

It was felt that there was no more fitting way to remember a loved one than by planting a living tree or grove. Over the years the tradition died out and it is now felt that it is time to revive it but to move the event to the Sunday in the Tree Council's National Tree Week which always starts in the last week of November. We see this as a chance not only to plant trees but to remember all the wonderful gifts that we receive from the bounty of the trees for whose creation we give thanks today.

Bidding Prayer

We are gathered here today to give thanks for the wonderful creation of the trees and all that they have done in the service of mankind. We remember: the warmth and shelter provided by logs and branches; the use of wooden boats on the water and wooden carts on the roads; the service of the wooden plough and the flour produced from the mill's wooden sails or water wheels; the wooden bowls and tankards that were placed on wooden tables to serve both food and drink; and the comfort of the wooden cot and wooden bed on which we rested. We give thanks for the fruits of the trees in their season, for the music created on instruments made from trees, and the great and boundless love shown to us all and symbolised by a wooden cross.

In these times of scientific awareness of the vital role of trees in sustaining all that is green and good on our planet we pray that the world will continue to increase the area of forest and woodland and that we may continue faithful stewards of the bounty with which we have been entrusted.

The Song of the Trees
This song was written by Alec and Doris Rowley in 1934 but the tune cannot be traced.

This is the song of England's trees,
The oak tree and the yew;
The chestnut with its flame of light
Shining against the blue.
The blue of Spring, the blue of lakes,
Forget-me-nots in streams;
The little silver birch trees,
Weaving their silver dreams.
Sweet are the birds of Britain's trees,
The oak tree and the yew,
The tiny buds and crinkled leaves,
All fresh and green and new.
The scent of spring in pink and white
Of twisted apple trees,
Where blossoms mingle happily,
With butterflies and bees.
All thro' the passing days and years,
The trees remain serene;
Each with its little offering,
Of joy clad all in green.
They give their shade,
Their Summer sounds,
And as the year departs,
They bow their lovely heads in gold,
And give their golden hearts.

A Reading
Isaiah 55, vv 8–13

Hymn
All things bright and beautiful
(Tune: Royal Oak)

A Reading
Revelations 21, vv 1–4,
22, vv 1–2

In Praise of Trees: Readings and Prayers

Without the oak
No beam in ship or hall;
Without the pine
No stately mast at all;
Without the elm
No barns to store the hay;
Without the chestnut
No conker games to play;
Without the walnut
No furniture of note;
Without the ash
No oars to row the boat.
Without the trees
No place to build a home
For nesting birds
When early Spring is come;
Without the trees
No blossom time to bring
From year to year The promises of Spring;
Without the trees
No shade in Summer heat;
Without the trees
No juicy fruit to eat.
We all need trees,
Protect them, please.

Vera Sinclair

He who plants a tree
He plants love,
Tents of coolness spreading out above
Wayfarers he may not live to see.
Gifts that grow are best;
Hands that bless are Blest;
Plant! Life does the rest.
Go forth in to the world in peace,

(Written for a service held on the first Armistice Day after the 1914–18 war at the Heritage Craft Schools and Home for Crippled Children, Chailey, Sussex)

Leader: Let us pray for all who plant and care for our trees.
For they shall be like a tree planted by the rivers of water, that bring forth their fruit in their season.

All: Their leaves shall not wither, and whatsoever they doeth shall prosper.

Leader: But the glory of the trees is more than their gifts,
'Tis a beautiful wonder of life that lifts
From a wrinkled seed in an earth-bound clod
A column, and arch in the Temple of God,
A pillar of power, a dome of delight,
A shine of song and a joy of sight.
Their leaves are alive with the breath of the earth,
They shelter the dwellings of man, and they bend
O'er his grave with the look of a loving friend.

All: They that plant a tree are the servants of God. They provide a kindness for many generations and faces that they have not seen will bless them.

Leader: We thank Thee, Lord, for the trees, Thy first great temples. Through the leafy windows of the woodland and forest glade stream the golden rays of sunlight. We see Thy presence in the majesty of the trees. May they forever be a reminder to us of those who saw them grow and are no more with us to enjoy the beauty of the earth. Let us feel our kinship with the trees as with all living things, and realise that we, and they, share this world as both givers and receivers of Grace. Help us to give our best to the world in which we live so that we may leave it a better and more beautiful place through our careful stewardship of Thy gifts. Lord, prosper the work of our planters, our foresters, our loggers and our carpenters that we may all work together to enjoy both the beauty of Thy creation and the fruits of our joint labours.

All: Amen

Hymn
As the beech within the wood,
As the pine upon the shore,
As the redwood in the forest
Rises from the shady floor;

Lord of life, please help us be
Strong and upright as a tree

As the hazel in the hedges,
As the hawthorn and the sloe
Give shelter to the shorn lamb
When the icy wet winds blow;
Lord of caring help us be
A source of comfort like a tree.

As the orchard's golden fruits,
As the orange and the pear,
Lime and lemon, nut and sap,
Feed Thy people everywhere,
Lord of bounty help us be
Full of succour as a tree

As the blossom of the cherry
And the acer's autumn glow,
As the aspen and the willow
When they whiten, row on row,
Lord of beauty let us be
Joy to all just like a tree.

As the dead tree on the hill
Into which the nails were driven
Turned a symbol of despair
To a sign of being forgiven,
Lord of love, please help us be
Signs of love, just like that tree

© National Memorial Arboretum

(Tune: 'England's Lane', Geoffrey Shaw, to 'For the beauty of the earth'. This hymn was written by David Childs for a tree planting in tribute to Lord Farnham, late President, The Tree Council.)

Reading
A version of Psalm 137 by Lord Byron

We sat down and wept by the waters
Of Babel, and thought of the day
When our foe, in the hue of his slaughters,
Made Salem's high places his prey;
And ye, oh her desperate daughters!
Were scattered all weeping away.

While sadly we gazed on the river
Which roll'd on in freedom below,
They demanded the song; but, oh never
That triumph the stranger shall know!
May this right hand be wither'd for ever,
Ere it string our high harp for the foe!

On this willow the harp is suspended,
Oh Salem! Its sound shall be free;
And the hour when thy glories were ended
But left me the token of thee:
And ne'er shall the soft tones be blended
With the voice of the spoiler by me!

Blessing
Be of good courage
Render to no man evil for evil
Strengthen the faint hearted
Support the weak
Love and serve the Lord

And may the joy of this day be yours
The joy of hearts and homes be yours
The joy of trees and the fruits of trees be yours
And the joy of the Father
The joy of the Son
And the joy of the Holy Spirit
Be with you and those whom you love
This day and for evermore

Amen

The congregation now move to the site of the tree planting

APPENDIX B

The Friends of the National Memorial Arboretum

After an exchange of correspondence in December 1997 Mrs Carol Davies-Lee of Alrewas organised an inaugural meeting of 'The Friends of The National Memorial Arboretum' on 25 March 1998. The meeting was attended by the following who became the first 'Friends' and assumed the roles on the Committee as indicated:

Carol Davies-Lee   Chairman
Roger Davies-Lee   Membership Secretary
Sylvia Kelly   Treasurer
Charles Elliott   Minutes Secretary
Julie Becket   Works Co-ordinator
Jackie Fisher   Publicity and Arboretum liaison
Anne Olphin
Lawrence Olphin   Legal Advisor
Sam Kent   Official photographer

and,
Sue Elliott
Ted and Maggie Brosch
John and Pat Croot
Penny Smith
Margaret Elliott
Margaret and John Middleton
Frank Kent

This small group was soon joined by Ralph and Maureen Rose (plaques), Bob and Muriel Morris (labelling of trees), Tony and Sue Critchley (education), Ann Smith (newsletter), Judith and Richard Thorpe (finance and wildlife), Roger Hailwood (talks), Ken Vaughan (site work), Ann Nolan (training), Maynard Scott (tours & Chapel talks), Les Wills (tours and talks), Pam Greenleaf (floral decoration), Laurie and Marie Walford, Derek van Arkadie, Jane Ault, Ken and Jane Vaughan, Ken, Margaret and Helen Pilgrim, Dennis and Jante Phillips (gardening and guiding). All of them undertook any jobs that needed doing as well as acting as guides.

By 2007 the number of Friends had passed 600.
The aims of the Friends, which were proposed by Carol and agreed by the committee were to:

a. bring knowledge of the Arboretum to a wider public
b. help practically where requested
c. offer help in manning the new building when opened
d. give guided tours to visiting groups
e. keep a record of activities as a history.

Both these and the constitution, which was agreed at the same time, remained in place for the first ten years.

In 2000 the Friends were successful in their own Lottery Application and purchased two motorised wheelchairs for visitors to the Arboretum. These were delivered in time for the official opening.

In October 1999 a uniform of sweatshirts and polo shirts were ordered so that Friends could be identified easily on the site.

After publicising the Arboretum at a number of local shows the Friends manned the Arboretum for the site's first major event, the unveiling of the Polar Bear. This was on 7 June 1998 and proved to be a great success. There was no Visitor Centre at the time but when that was eventually opened the Friends took on the additional roles of running the kitchen, serving at and clearing tables and washing up. Without their willing involvement such events would have been impossible to stage.

After the Polar Bear's unveiling the Founder wrote to the Friends stating that 'the fact that we can rely on the support of the Friends on these occasions is a great source of relief and pride'.

That remains true and the Friends have been attending events and working at Arboretum ever since.

In the Chapel the Friends provide a guide every day of the year and organise an Epiphany Service which now fills the building.

The success of the Friends is due not only to a shared vision but to the fact that they have become a family, enjoying socialising and days out away from the site as well as working at it. Gather any group of them together and what is heard the most is laughter.

The Arboretum could not have progressed so far so smoothly without them.

The Wildlife at the Arboretum

The National Memorial Arboretum, situated as it is on the banks of two major rivers which act as migratory routes, is rich in wildlife. The improvement of the water quality by the active intervention of the Environment Agency is best illustrated by the return of otters to the rivers. The resident creatures and their habitat have been audited, studied and brought to the attention of visitors by Richard Thorpe who runs wildlife tours of the site. The list below is just an indication of the joy that this wildlife brings.

Birds

A wide collection of species including:

Blackbird, blackcap, black-headed gull, blue tit, buzzard, Canada goose, chaffinch, chiffchaff, collared dove, common tern, coot, cormorant, crow, dunlin, dunnock, fieldfare, garden warbler, goldeneye, goldfinch, goosander, great crested grebe, great spotted woodpecker, great tit, greenfinch, green woodpecker, grey wagtail, heron, herring gull, hobby, house martin, kestrel, kingfisher, lapwing, lesser black backed gull, linnet, little owl, little ringed plover, long tailed tit, magpie, mallard, meadow pipit, mistle thrush, moorhen, mute swan, oystercatcher, partridge, pheasant, pied wagtail, redshank, redwing, reed bunting, ringed plover, robin, rook, sand martin, sedge warbler, shelduck, short eared owl, skylark, snipe, song thrush, starling, stock dove, stonechat, swallow, swift, teal, tufted duck, wheatear, whitethroat, widgeon, willow tit, willow warbler, wood pigeon, wren, yellow wagtail.

Rare visitors have included a hoopoe and a black redstart.

Mallards have twice raised young in the War Widows' Rose Garden.

Visitors love the skylarks and the many fly-pasts of geese and swans. The sound of skylarks singing during the 2 minute silence is an experience never to be forgotten for many visitors.

Mammals

Fox, badger, brown hare, wood mouse, bank vole, shrew, weasel, stoat, pipistrelle bat, Daubentons bat, rabbit, otter, mink, brown rat.

The sighting of a hare by visitors is always special.

Otter surveys have found evidence of otters. Various mammal surveys have been done and are a very popular activity with visitors young and old, providing the opportunity to see and touch live creatures.

Similarly, bat walks by the River Tame at dusk with the use of bat detectors are popular.

Fish in River Tame

Eel, roach, perch, chub, pike, identified by recent Environment Agency electro fishing.

Insects

Many species of moths, butterflies, damselflies, and dragonflies.

The attractive blue-banded demoiselle damselfly is particularly numerous along the river banks during the summer months.

Aquatic life in ponds

Several pond dipping sessions by children have discovered a great variety of beasties, including pond skaters, water boatmen, tadpoles, diving beetles and dragonfly nymphs.

The Northern Ireland Stone Circle

(Information courtesy of Aardvark Geological Service)

Antrim: The boulder, which weighs just under 12 tonnes, was supplied by Loughside Quarries. The rock is Dolerite, an igneous rock, which reached the surface about 65 million years ago. The rock type is similar and roughly contemporary with the Giant's Causeway and forms part of a massive series of volcanic centres that marked the formation of the Atlantic Ocean during the Tertiary period. The rock forming the boulder was part of a series of lava flows which covered most of County Antrim. Although it cooled sufficiently slowly to form fairly large tightly interlocking crystals, which are visible on fresh surfaces of the rock, the cooling was not sufficiently slow to produce the hexagonal tension cracking which gives the columns of the Giant's Causeway their distinctive shape.

Down: The boulder was supplied by John Finlay, Carrowdore Quarry and weighs just under 12 tonnes. The rock is a Greywacke and was deposited as a jumbled mix of clays and sands on the floor of the Iapetus Ocean during the Silurian period (417 to 443 million years ago). The collision between the southern and northern parts of what became the British Isles about 400 million years ago compressed and folded the ocean floor sediment to form the hard compact rock of the boulder. The original layers can still be identified by changes in the grain size between bands within the rock and the bending and folding effects of the collision are partially preserved by the white bands of secondary quartz which have infilled the cracks.

Armagh: This boulder was provided by W G Mills & Son and is composed of Carboniferous Limestone laid down in the Visean age (333-352 million years ago). The rock started out as a lime-rich mud in the warm shallow seas that covered Ireland at the time. Burial and time caused re-crystallisation of the lime to form a hard crystalline rock in which individual calcite crystals can be identified. Cracks and fracture from earth movements are gradually sealed up by deposition of calcite from the groundwater giving the extensive fine white secondary veining visible throughout the boulder.

Fermanagh: This 7 tonne limestone boulder, supplied by B McCaffrey & Sons, is also of the Visean age and was deposited when Northern Ireland lay just north of the equator. The water had minor amounts of iron in solution and this was deposited along with the limestone to give a markedly pink colour to the resultant limestone. The transformation of the soft lime-rich muds into stone results in large amounts of lime being dissolved out and insoluble clays remaining behind to form the rather distinctive darker stylolite forming the upper surface of this block.

Tyrone: The 8 tonne Tyrone boulder was quarried from an Upper Devonian (360–374 million years old) suite of rocks in the Fintona Block. It is a conglomerate made up mainly from a red-brown medium of coarse quartz grains coloured by iron oxide indicating a dry desert origin. The rock also contains large rounded pebbles of quartz and igneous rocks. The presence of fine sand and coarse pebbles means that the material was not laid down by wind, which is how most desert sandstones are formed, but was formed in the floors of a wadi by flash floods.

Londonderry: W & J Chambers supplied this 8 tonne block of Dalradian Metasediments which was laid down some 600 million years ago near the south pole, making it the oldest rock in the Ashgrove. Deep burial and intense folding during the Caledonian orogeny (510-430 years ago) transformed the sediments into a mix of mica schists and quartzite and produced the complex patterning visible on the surfaces of the boulder. The distinctive silver fleck on the surface is the mica and the wavy banding is the result of folding of the individual layers. The quartzites and secondary quartz veining shows up as the very hard white bands.

The granite pillar and seats: The 3 metre tall pillar and the seats are cut from Mourne Granite, a Tertiary age (circa 65 million year ago) igneous complex associated with the opening of the Atlantic Ocean. Unlike the Antrim dolerite the magma in this case did not reach the surface but cooled over a period of several million years at a depth of 3 to 5 kilometres below the surface. The slow cooling, combined with the chemistry of the magma, produced a strong interlocking mixture of quartz feldspar and mica grains that give the characteristic salt and pepper appearance of the granite. The flat smooth surfaces are produced by slicing the large quarried blocks with diamond tipped saw blades: the rough faces are the result of the quarry men splitting the stone out of the side of the mountain where the quarry is situated.

Gravel surround: This attractive pink gravel was supplied by Norman Emerson & Sons and contains a mixture of granites, schists, dolerite, quartzite and sandstone from a fluvio-glacial deposit from County Tyrone. Melting of the glaciers which covered Northern Ireland some 8,000 to 10,000 years ago gave rise to massive floods which flushed out much stone from the wide range present in the Sperrin Mountains. The tumbling action of the water rounded the sharp edges to form a gravel.

Bibliography

The design and development of the National Memorial Arboretum involved much consultation in books of reference and accounts of campaigns to ensure that the design of each plot was appropriate for the group for whom it was being created. This bibliography, however, contains suggested reading for anyone who is mindful to find out more about the events that led to the individual plots being established. It is, therefore, set out by plot rather than the more traditional alphabetical order by author.

Leonard Cheshire
Morris, R, *Cheshire*, Viking, 2000

Royal Navy
Roskill, Captain S., *The War at Sea 1939–1945*, London, 1958

Army
Hallows, I. S., *Regiments and Corps of the British Army*, New Orchard, 1994

Merchant Navy
Woodman R., *The Real Cruel Sea: the Merchant Navy in the Battle of the Atlantic*, John Murray, 2004
Macintyre, D., *The Battle of the Atlantic*, Pan, 1969
Slader, J., *The Fourth Service – Merchantmen at War 1939–45*, Robert Hale, 1994
Menzies, J, *Children of the Doomed Voyage*, Wiley, 2005
Nagorski, T., *Miracles on the Water*, Hyperion, 2006

Royal Air Force
Bishop, P., *Bomber Boys*, Harper, 2007
Bishop, P., *Fighter Boys*, Harper, 2004
Hasting, M., *Bomber Command*, Michael Joseph, 1979
Kershaw, A., *The Few*, Penguin, 2006
Oliver, K. M., *Through Adversity, the official history of the RAF Regiment*

Polar Bear
Pell, C. R., *Tigers Never Sleep*, 1994

Dunkirk
Gallico, P., *The Snow Goose*, Penguin
Lord, W., *The Miracle of Dunkirk*, Allen Lane, 1983
Sebag-Montefiore, H., *Dunkirk, Fight to the Last Man*, Viking, 2006

Burma Campaign
Hill, J., *Slim's Burma Boys*, Spillmount, 2007
Fraser, G. MacDonald, *Quartered Safe Out Here*, Harvill, 1992
Hill, J., *Slim's Burma Boys*, Spillmount, 2007
Latimer, J., *Burma, the Forgotten War*, John Murray, 2004
Thompson, J., *War in Burma, 1942-1945*, Sidgwick & Jackson, 2002

Far East Prisoners of War
Allan, S., *Diary of a Girl in Changi*, Kangaroo Press, 1999
Lomax, E., *The Railway Man*, Vintage, 1996
King, C., *River Kwai Railway*, Brasseys, 1992
Searle, R., *To the Kwai and Back*, Souvenir, 1986
Seiker, F., *Lest We Forget*, Bevere Vivis, 1995

Mediterranean
Harrison, F., *Tobruk*, Brockhampton, 1999
Holland, J., *Fortress Malta*, Orion, 2003
MacDonald, C., *The Lost Battle*, MacMillan, 1993
Moorhead, A., *Gallipoli*, Wordsworth, 1997
Thomas, D., *Crete 1941*, Andre Deutsch, 1972

Korea
Hastings, M., *The Korean War*, Michael Joseph, 1987
Hickey, M., *Korean War*, John Murray, 1999

Normandy
Hastings, M., *Overlord*, Michael Joseph, 1984

National Service
Hickman, T., *The Call-Up*, Headline, 2004
Thomas, L., *The Virgin Soldiers*, Constable, 1966
Walker, A., *A Barren Place: National Servicemen in Korea*, Pen & Sword, 1954
Wesker, A., *Chips with Everything*, Jonathan Cape, 1962

Ulster
McKittrick, D. et al, *Lost Lives*, Mainstream, 1999
Restorick, Rita, *Death of a Soldier*, Black Staff, 2000

Victoria Cross
De La Billiere, P., *Supreme Courage*, Little Brown, 2004
Sebag-Montefiore, H., *The Victoria Cross*, Enigma, Viking, 2000

Shot at Dawn
Corns, C. & Hughes-Wilson, J., *Blindfold and Alone*, Cassells, 2001
Putkowski, J. and Sykes, J., *Shot at Dawn*, Pen & Sword, 1989

Trees
Gibbons, B., *Trees*, Reed Consumer, 1991
Kelly, J., ed., *The Hillier Guide to Trees & Shrubs*, David & Charles, 1995
Leathart, S., *Whence our Trees*, Foulsham, 1991
Mabey, R., *Flora Britannica*, Chatto & Windus, 1996
Miles, A., *Silva*, Ebury, 1999
Mitchell, A., *Trees of Britain*, Harper Collins, 1996
Mitchell, A. & Coombes, A., *The Garden Tree*, Weidenfeld & Nicolson, 1998
Royal Horticultural Society, *Garden Trees*, Dorling Kindersley, 1996
Rushforth, K., *Conifers*, Helm, 1987

Index